SPELLCASTING

beyond the basics

About the Author

Michael Furie (Northern California) is the author of *Spellcasting for Beginners* and *Supermarket Magic*, both published by Llewellyn. He has been a practicing Witch for over twenty years. An American Witch by tradition, he practices in the Irish tradition and is a priest of the Cailleach. You can find him online at www.michaelfurie.com.

To Write to the Author

If you wish to contact the author or would like more information about this book, please write to the author in care of Llewellyn Worldwide, and we will forward your request. Both the author and publisher appreciate hearing from you and learning of your enjoyment of this book and how it has helped you. Llewellyn Worldwide cannot guarantee that every letter written to the author can be answered, but all will be forwarded. Please write to:

Michael Furie
℅ Llewellyn Worldwide
2143 Wooddale Drive
Woodbury, MN 55125-2989

Please enclose a self-addressed stamped envelope for reply or $1.00 to cover costs. If outside the USA, enclose an international postal reply coupon instead.

THE NEXT STEPS
TO BETTER MAGIC

SPELLCASTING

beyond the basics

Michael Furie

Llewellyn Worldwide
Woodbury, Minnesota

FIRST EDITION
First Printing, 2016

Book design by Bob Gaul
Cover design by Kevin R. Brown
Cover images by iStockphoto.com/57328162/© tarczas
             Shutterstock.com/179477522/©Happy MIA
Editing by Laura Graves
Interior art by Llewellyn art department

Llewellyn Publications is a registered trademark of Llewellyn Worldwide Ltd.

Library of Congress Cataloging-in-Publication Data
Names: Furie, Michael, 1978–
Title: Spellcasting beyond the basics : the next steps to better magic/
Michael Furie.
Includes bibliographical references and index.
Subjects: LCSH: Magic. | Charms.
Classification: LCC BF1621 (print)
DDC   133.4/4—dc23
ISBN: 9780738745534

Llewellyn Publications
A Division of Llewellyn Worldwide Ltd.
2143 Wooddale Drive
Woodbury, MN 55125-2989
www.llewellyn.com

Printed in the United States of America

To Dray, to my family and my friends, many thanks for the love, support, and advice. Blessed be.

Contents

PART TWO: Magical Practice

PART THREE: Ingredients & Recipes

Introduction

In my previous book, *Spellcasting for Beginners,* the basics of magic were explained—what magic is and a variety of spells designed to harness and direct that power. While this is not exactly a direct sequel to that book, it does venture a bit beyond the basics. It isn't necessary to be a practicing Witch or even to have read my earlier work, but it is a good idea to know basic magical procedures such as casting a circle, setting up an altar, dressing candles, and timing magic according to the moon phases. Experience with things like candle spells and visualization is helpful too. Even still, I have tried to incorporate enough basic material to offer a starting place for any practitioner so that *Spellcasting: Beyond the Basics* is wholly inclusive in itself.

This book goes deeper into the practice, answering such questions as: "How does magic really work?" and "How do I work with familiars?" It includes further expansion of the structure of ritual, how to *really* do things like psychic influence using a scrying mirror as a window to the Otherworld, and how to become truly spiritually centered—probably the most important goal of any spiritual practice. This book also contains loads of new spells and rituals that were a bit too advanced for a beginner's book. The text is not only a deeper exploration of the material presented in previous work, but also a foray into other areas of magical life such as remote viewing and why Witches work outdoor rituals around bonfires and trees.

Topics that will be covered include such things as merging with the elements, shifting consciousness through the different brainwave levels from beta down through to delta; how the stars, planets, and zodiac can play significant roles in spell work; ancient metaphysical laws and tenets concerning the natures of energy and matter; and how to use all this knowledge for the benefit of yourself and others. Lesser used practices such as sending out etheric tendrils, creating a "nocturnal servitor," and weather magic (often considered taboo) are covered with working methods as well as the potential goals for these techniques. Both protective and defensive magic are examined as well as healing and strengthening work, psychic development and divination, and of course the two most (arguably) frequent magical goals—love and money.

This book is divided into three parts: magical theory, magical practice, and ingredients and recipes. As magic is a natural art that uses spiritual forces, the magical theory section covers topics such as the different forms of manifestation work; techniques for self-awareness and meditation; altered states of consciousness; connecting to the natural world; planetary and stellar information; and the Hermetic laws that aim to describe how matter, energy, and thought operate within the universe and how this knowledge can be used in magical practice. The beauty is that once these lessons are taken to heart, even the simplest spell becomes a more advanced working as the way magic is approached becomes fuller and richer in depth.

The section on magical practice covers all the practical techniques and spells with chapters divided by intention. There are classic rituals and methods included as well as special spells such as the Princess and the Pea ritual and the Elements of Self-Esteem rite to provide a variety of options for different magical goals.

The final section includes the recipes and herbal information for the different oils, incenses, and potions called for in the book's spells and rituals. Following is a Latin name (scientific genus species) cross reference, a full index, and bibliography. If you have practiced magic for a while and find yourself yearning for more—expansion into the wider magical world—I hope you will find this a welcome guide.

PART ONE
Magical Theory

This section moves into intermediate magical training topics such as timing, intent, emotion, focus, energy raising, and projection. It also covers broader topics such as integrating magic into our regular lives and how to shift our consciousness into different brainwave states at will. Planetary magic, natural laws, aura viewing, transplanting of consciousness, and the structure of ritual is covered in this section, but before we can understand how to best use the variety of energy and power at our fingertips, we must first know the ways in which magic brings about manifestation.

ONE

Know Your Magic

We begin with magic's more subtle processes, including the different types of magical manifestation. We will examine how to best activate and empower magical work for maximum effectiveness. To begin, let's look at a general guideline showing *how* magic can manifest our desire in the physical world.

How Does Magic Work?

As I have stated in previous work, my definition of magic is: "Magic is the science and process of projecting emotionally and intellectually charged energy into the spiritual plane in order to manifest change in the physical world. Even though that defines it, it doesn't really explain how it works, does it? There are many varied theories about exactly how it works and in my experience, it usually works in the following manner:

- I decide on a magical goal and prepare for the spell.

- I go through all the steps, gathering what is necessary and beginning the rite; connecting with allies and deities when appropriate.

- I raise power through a pre-chosen method.

- I imprint upon the power my desired outcome. If I am working with one, I use that power to charge whatever tool or focus called for in the spell (one that is properly aligned to my goal).

- Work the spell and release the energy; projecting it to my goal, the Otherworld, allies, or deities depending on the nature of the spell and my magical goal.

- Ground the excess energy.

- The programmed power I have released goes into the astral plane (or to the allies or deities) and manifests the goal on that level. It creates an astral form of the desired goal.

- The physical plane (since it is essentially a condensed manifestation of the astral) begins to change and align with my magical goal. And finally,

- The goal manifests in the physical world of form.

This is a very basic and general interpretation of how magic works. For spells that are meant to affect people rather than alter situations, it works a little differently.

Usually the power is sent directly toward the person and is considered to affect first the astral self and then filter into the subconscious mind almost like post-hypnotic suggestion, causing different behavior in accordance with the spell caster's desire. Of course it is difficult to use magic on another person as their own natural shielding and willpower automatically resist outside influence. It is also very likely that the spell will rebound on the spell caster causing anxiety and tension in them, at the very least. Many Witches consider it bad form to cast spells *on* people unless extreme circumstances are involved. It is much wiser (and safer) to alter situations rather than try to dominate and overwhelm another person's free will; the latter is predatory and selfish behavior that usually brings back only trouble. Some exceptions exist, and all Witches must come to terms with the ethical implications of such magic in their own hearts and minds before deciding to engage in this kind of work. When a person is causing harm and will continue unchecked in this harmful behavior, a Witch may choose to magically intervene with a binding spell to restrict the harmful person's actions either to make it so he or she is caught by authorities or to stop the ability to engage in the behaviors.

Depending on the strength of the harmful person's will, a single Witch may not be able to bind the person successfully. More than one Witch or perhaps a full coven would have to agree to the work. Needless to say, this type of magic does not occur very often. Most magical work focuses on healing, protection, love, and prosperity and abundance. Magic's major goals will be addressed in part 2 in further detail, but for now I'd like to talk about the two major methods used to work magic: affinity manifestation and creation manifestation.

Different Types of Magic

The first of the two major ways to work magic is known as affinity manifestation, or working with the law of attraction. Using this method, energy is sent out to draw an outcome toward the spell caster. It is a good basic method and is probably the most common form of magical practice. A typical mode of employing affinity manifestation is the use of charms designed to attract something (such as good luck or money) or someone (such as a new love or business contacts).

These attraction charms work such that each ingredient—aligned with the magical goal—is charged with energy and intention by the spell caster to radiate influence around the wearer so that energy is attuned to attract the desire. In magical terms: like attracts like, and magical energy operates in a similar fashion to gravity, in this respect. As with gravity, the greater amount of particles that join together, the greater the force of attraction becomes. The expression of gravitational force is most evident in relation to the planets. Generally speaking, the larger the planet, the larger its gravity; the smaller the planet, the lesser its gravity.

Taking magnetic force into consideration, we know that opposites attract. There is some magical significance to it as well (some of the deeper aspects of the interaction of opposing magical energies is covered in chapter 4). In affinity manifestation, any energy that would act as opposition to the chosen magical goal is usually neutralized, transformed, or warded away to keep only the energies aligned with the magical goal. In this way, everything in the charm emits the same frequency and is passed on to the bearer so his or her own energies (aura) begins to resonate with this same frequency which further attracts more of the same energies and of course, those people or situations which carry those energies, thus fulfilling the magical desire.

Most magical products such as magical oils, incense, and charms are instruments of affinity manifestation; they are designed to attract or neutralize/repel a specific force or intention. In the case of neutralizing an opposing (or undesired) force, the affinity magic works to alter the vibration of the unwanted energy along its polarity so it is no longer harmful or disruptive much like an antacid medicine is used as a heartburn remedy. On the other hand, affinity-based work designed to repel something tends to work through deflection. The magic creates a spiritual barrier preventing the disruptive energy from making contact with the person. Much like an umbrella bears the brunt of a rain shower; the magic keeps us from being drenched in unwanted energy. The affinity is that our magical object aligns to our goal of protection/deflection, and its nature would be opposite to the force we wish to repel, thus blocking its ability to gain access to our aura or environment where it can cause problems.

When using affinity manifestation magic (magical items or no), it is important to remember to keep things relatively general. Using magic intended to draw something to you carries with it the understanding that the thing one desires already exists in some form somewhere. The more conditions placed in a spell on the form in which we wish our goal to manifest, the more difficult it will be for the spell to be effective. If the goal (thing, person, event, etc.) already exists, it exists as is under its own power—attaching too many conditions to our magical goal may hinder success.

As an example, let's say I'm seeking new friends and create a charm bag designed to draw potential friends to me. I work the spell on a Friday during a waxing moon when the moon is traveling through Aquarius (the astrological sign most associated with friendship). At my work table I write out a short list of qualities I wish any potential friends to possess on a small square of new paper. When I am ready to begin, I light a pink candle charged with my desire for new friends, burn some rose petals on a charcoal tablet as incense, and fill a pink charm bag with a rose quartz, some dried lemon peel, dried pink rose petals, dried sweet pea blossoms, and the list of qualities I have written. I charge the bag with my energy and intent and tie the bag shut with pink or white cord. The bag is then carried with me wherever I go.

Now the way the friendship spell would usually work is that the charm would attune my aura to the same frequency of the people who possess the qualities I have specified. When I encounter such people, we would naturally be drawn to each other since our energies would be compatible. This is where being somewhat general comes in handy. If, for example, my list of qualities a friend must have contained: Pagan, 30 to 40 years old, nonsmoker, and vegetarian, it would automatically eliminate many people who do not fit those criteria, but a large enough pool of people remains. But if my list said: Pagan, 35 years old, nonsmoker, vegetarian, tall, blond, plays guitar, loves shopping, and loves dogs and cats, it would exclude a great many more people—the more conditions I add, the less likely it is that anyone will possess all the necessary qualities. It is a better idea for me to consider the qualities I prefer and whittle the list down to the absolutely essential traits, the "deal breakers," and to work the magic with the intention of drawing the "correct" friends to me. In this way, I do not unintentionally eliminate potentially good friends by having too narrow a scope in my spell work. Affinity manifestation is very good and effective magic, and it can work wonders in our lives, but it is only one of a Witch's many magical skills. The second form of manifestation is a bit more advanced and difficult: it is creation manifestation.

I touched on the concept of creation manifestation in my book *Supermarket Magic* as an extension of the human will. For comparison: while in affinity manifestation energy is sent out essentially as a beacon and magnet to draw something to you, in creation manifestation you are sending energy out to astrally *create* some thing or situation which then manifests in the material plane, as the physical is a manifestation of the astral. Since we are all a part of the same divine energy, we all have a similar (though more limited) capacity for creation as our creators. When we release energy from ourselves into the astral plane with the intent of creating and manifesting a part of ourselves as a particular quality we wish to embody, we imprint our intent on the astral plane. When properly projected, the intention gathers astral energy to form around it, strengthening it and causing it to fully form on that plane. And when the intention has taken root in the astral, it begins to move into the physical plane because the physical world is itself a condensed manifestation of the astral plane. Once the intention has condensed into the physical, our goal is made manifest.

The foundation of this level of magic is a change in perception. When choosing to perceive something such as creating an image in our mind's eye, it is a part of us. When we project that energy out into the astral plane for manifestation, we are essentially manifesting a part of ourselves; we move our energy and intention outward to reach the magical goal, shifting from merely existing in the universe as passive bystanders to being active participants in its creation. A prime reason for working in this way is that it removes the subconscious barrier that exists when working solely with the law of attraction: the perception of lack.

In the moment when you ask for something, you have instantly acknowledged that you do not yet have it. That acknowledgment creates the feeling of lack which in turn can act as a hindrance to the manifestation of your goal. It is far more productive to feel (and speak) as though what you want has already manifested. The feeling is the most important component of the process. Our words declare to ourselves what we desire and clarify our intention *to us,* but in order to send the message outward to actually create the change we seek, we must communicate through image and emotion. Spoken language is itself secondary, a thing done primarily for the spellcaster's benefit. To truly touch the Universal Mind, the Goddess, the God, and to imprint our desire into the astral plane for it to be mirrored back to us in the physical realm, it is necessary to project the energy of our desire through the vehicles of image and feeling.

Essentially, you must feel as though your goal has already been reached and you must feel the goal itself. If, for example, you are working for rain (weather magic will be covered in greater detail in chapter 13), it is best to visualize that it is raining right at that moment and you can hear and feel the rain. Try to conjure up not only a mental image but also the physical sensations of standing out in the rain; feel it against your skin, hear the sound of the raindrops hitting the ground, and inhale the petrichor of a rainy day. As you are holding this concept in your mind, also add the feeling you wish to have as the result of this rain whether it be joy, relief, satisfaction, or gratitude; whatever it is, infuse it into your magical mental construct and build its strength. When you have reached the peak of this image, when you actually feel (for however brief a moment) that the goal has indeed manifested, the energy can then be released to achieve the goal.

Any words that would be added to the spell to define your intent would also serve an important purpose. There is great power in the written and spoken word, and much of it is in setting up clear parameters for the spell so that it does not unfold in inappropriate or unwelcome ways. Some energy travels on the breath, so the act of speaking a spell can help project the energy outward so that the spell is cast. The energy must first be programmed with the mental and emotional imagery described above in order for the magic to be effective, however. Additionally, magical products such as incense and oils that work according to affinity manifestation can be used as energy enhancers to keep a spell properly focused. Spells are together a rich tapestry that must be woven with genuine drive and passion for success to be achieved.

For the necessary drive that generates that magical spark needed to create change, it is imperative that we operate from our true selves. And to operate as our true selves, we need to know ourselves well and be spiritually centered beings.

TWO

Know Yourself

As Shakespeare wrote, "This above all: to thine own self be true"—but first you have to really know who you are before you know *how* to be true to yourself. It is so important for us as spiritual, magically-minded people that we know who we are, what we think, and how we feel about the world at a deep and profound level. When we work magic, we are projecting our desires into the external world. If we are bogged down subconsciously with self-doubt or low self-esteem our results can be hit-or-miss or nonexistent. It is important that we free ourselves from clouded judgment and the weight of culturally imposed beliefs to reach the true essence of what we feel and how we view the world. Honesty is key to this process; we must be honest about our feelings and inner natures both positive and negative. This type of deep self-examination is the beginning of the transformative effort known as *shadow work*.

Self Awareness

The first step in shadow work is to examine what we think and how we feel about the big questions and our place in the world (easier said than done, of course). As an example, you can make lists of beliefs you hold such as where you stand on social, religious, or political issues (they can be short, like a "top ten most important beliefs about an issue" or a more lengthy extended one) and then study the lists, contemplating why you believe what you do. Many times, we hold beliefs simply because we trusted someone else's opinion. While this isn't necessarily a bad thing—they may indeed be right about the issue—it is a very good idea to consider our beliefs in a detached and unbiased context and investigate to find our own personal answers behind our beliefs. In doing so, we can be sure of ourselves and stand firmly in our truth. As most good teachers will tell you, don't believe anything just because someone said it—believe something based on your own experiences.

Another valuable exercise is to make two more lists, one with all the positive qualities that you have such as "good listener," "hard working," or "compassionate," and another with negative qualities such as "tendency to procrastinate," "lazy," bossy," and so on. Examine each list carefully and be honest with yourself. Check to see if any of the negative qualities should instead be on the positive list; is "lazy" really a negative quality? Also check the positive qualities to see if any are secretly negative traits: is "totally honest" really just an excuse to insult others with harsh words? After any revisions have been made, study both lists. Confronting your shadow self—your negative traits—can be a difficult process, but it is usually very rewarding. Gradually, work can be done over time to correct the negative traits. Once the negative aspects have been corrected, they can be crossed off the list and the newly acquired positive traits can be written on the positive list.

Keep in mind that "positive" and "negative" are not used here to indicate good and evil but rather to describe traits we are comfortable with that seem to enrich our lives and interpersonal relationships (positive) and those that seem to detract from our lives and relationships (negative). More specifically, as we move through life we are continually changing, learning, and evolving not only as individuals but also as members of the larger community, a progression that necessitates adjustments in our perceptions and expression of the self. If this were not so, we might all still view the world through the eyes of a toddler. The either/or style of black and white thinking predominant at that stage of life would severely undermine the complicated negotiations and compromise necessary in adulthood.

There are instances where displaying what could be considered positive traits of being a giving and helpful person could result in over-depletion of resources or aiding a destructive individual, which is actually harmful. Additionally, sometimes it is very necessary to maintain so-called negative traits for a variety of reasons such as self-defense, and there should be no shame attached to this. Confronting our shadow side is not about "conquer and destroy" where we seek to vanquish our negative qualities and exist in a static state of idealized purity or goodness. There must be balance. Our personalities and self-awareness are ever-changing, and that is the beauty of the human experience. We are not frozen in time, bound to our original perspectives without a choice; we have the ability to change. The most crucial facet of self-awareness is not in pinning down an immutable catalog of qualities in order to be "complete" but rather to recognize that we each have within ourselves the power of transformation; we have been gradually transforming throughout our lives and once acknowledged, we can begin to consciously shape these changes so that we may become more self-directed individuals. The key is the process. Understanding of the self is a tricky thing as is trying to even define it, but operating from a place of love, compassion, and integrity helps us move forward in this work so we may begin to find our center.

Being Spiritually Centered

Being a spiritually centered person is a matter of shifting from being focused only on the mundane and the physical toward a more multidimensional viewpoint (no pun intended) with acknowledgement of the spiritual aspects of life and our connection to all things. One of the reasons for examining personal beliefs and positive and negative personality traits is that one of the paths to becoming spiritually centered is being free of inner conflict. Being spiritually centered is a powerful tool allowing us to truly embrace who we are as people and how we approach life. If you study spiritual gurus or masters of any faith, one key factor presents itself repeatedly: they practice what they preach. In other words, they live their lives according to a set of clearly defined beliefs adhered to without exception. There is no room for inner conflict or hypocrisy.

Psychologists have identified a state known as cognitive dissonance, defined by the American Psychological Association as:

> ...a state of despair induced when a person holds two contradictory beliefs, or when a belief is incongruent with an action that the person had chosen freely to perform. Because this situation produces feelings of discomfort, the individual strives to change one of the beliefs or behaviors in order to avoid being inconsistent. Hypocrisy is a special case of cognitive dissonance, produced when a person freely chooses to promote a behavior that they do not themselves practice.

I believe cognitive dissonance to be one of the greatest social ills in human society. When people feel driven to hold a belief because it was instilled in them as a child but they personally feel that the belief is either too restrictive or wholly invalid as an adult, frustration and dissatisfaction with life builds within the mind. We've seen the results of unrelenting cognitive dissonance on a societal scale many times in the past.

When a group—we'll use the Puritans as an example—is compelled to hold personally restrictive beliefs that are too difficult for even themselves to comply with, the result is a feeling like a gnawing sense of inadequacy, guilt, and despair, now known as cognitive dissonance. The result is a large number of spiritually, mentally, emotionally, and physically unfulfilled people (which I guess is fine if that's their choice). When they encounter another group of people who practices a different set of beliefs (in the case of Puritans, that could be Native Americans; Pagans; less restrictive Christians; anybody, really...) and those people appear happier and more fulfilled than the former group, the inner conflict only grows. To ease this conflict they have only three possible courses of action: isolate themselves from the less restrictive people and continue in their ways, change their own restrictive beliefs and live a more relaxed life, or persecute those living more freely than they, in order to reinforce their own sense of values and ease some of their secret feelings of inadequacy.

Sadly, this last choice seems to be the most popular one. Far too many people throughout history have mistaken the sense of power felt when they convert people to their beliefs for true spirituality and religious fulfillment. Instead of becoming spiritually centered themselves, they choose to force their values on others, attempting to stamp out other belief systems in the hope that it reinforces and "proves" the supremacy and truth of their own beliefs to themselves. If a person believes that inner conflict and a feeling of spiritual emptiness are the way it must be, they are living in needless misery and becoming potentially dangerous to any around them who do not share in their narrow outlook.

To become spiritually centered, it is vital that we operate from our true selves. To hold any belief only because someone else claimed it as fact gives up of personal control. A belief should only be held if, upon personal examination and experimentation you find it truly speaks to you and enriches your life. When considering the beliefs on the lists made earlier, any shame or fear-based beliefs must be thoroughly examined. Truly determine whether or not any guilt, shame, fear, or self-doubt is based on genuine wrongs you may have committed or if it is based on unfair labels and projections placed on you by others. The journey of spiritual centerdness will no doubt be an emotional one but I assure you it is definitely worthwhile. Depending on the nature and severity of any emotional issues, therapy may be required to properly resolve them. I would recommend it but use your best judgment. Just remember that we are all human, prone to mistakes. One of the great challenges in life is to learn from and grow beyond our mistakes. Let go of shame and fear.

It is necessary to work through and eliminate any conflicting or hypocritical beliefs. As previously mentioned, hypocrisy is another form of cognitive dissonance that will continue to keep you away from your centered self. Remember the difference between being able to see both perspectives in an argument and never being able to give a singular personal opinion on anything because you don't feel able to take a definitive stance on any issue. The latter results from continuing to hold conflicting beliefs that keep you bound in shame and guilt and blur the lines so you can't find personal truth. When you are centered, you are able to live your truth and when appropriate, speak it with a clear and proud voice because you know deep within your heart that it is your truth and you will be unwilling to abandon it.

Once all your beliefs align, the next important step in becoming centered is actually living according to those beliefs. Remember that it is just as important to "do" as it is to understand and feel. There are three aspects to our personalities: thinking, willing, and feeling. We need to use all three as equally as possible in order to live fully. Thinking and (hopefully) feeling have been involved in the process so far, but never forget the power of the human will. Magically speaking, it is connected to the fire element, and it is that special spark only gained through actual experience; contemplation, evaluation, intellectual understanding, and emotional connection are only parts of the process. To be complete, we must practice what we preach.

Taken as a whole, the process of understanding and nurturing the self cannot be completed overnight. Consider, however, the rewards of operating from your true self: you become much more self-assured and develop the core spiritual strength that is the foundation of inner peace. To become spiritually centered isn't just about confronting the shadow self and transforming negative traits—we must develop an awareness of and a relationship with the spiritual side of life. It is important to know that numerous things exist beyond our perception via our five senses. We are spiritual beings housed in physical bodies.

It is very beneficial to cultivate a balanced view of love and power. Love is nonjudgmental and nonmanipulative. When we have the ability to love freely without conditions or desperation, we gain the ability to truly move forward and connect to the loving energy of the universe. Power is usually viewed as control or as responsibility. People who view power as some form of control tend to be more aggressive and less spiritual, at least in my experience. This view of power is through the lens of force, war, authority, and conquest. In and of themselves, none of these things are inherently wrong or bad, but they relate more to division and demarcation whereas spirituality is more attuned to merging and blending. When power is viewed as responsibility, such as the responsibility to maintain the well-being of one's family or home, keeping a business profitable, or even cultivating a garden, it becomes much more about caring and consideration. In each of these examples exists the choice to continue in the endeavor. If the person responsible were to choose not to continue, the situation would be drastically altered for everyone else involved, yet when the idea of power is viewed in this way, things usually never become about controlling anyone else but instead remain focused on facilitating benefit and growth.

All of this centers around moving away from a narrow focus and to a larger world view; seeing the innate spirituality and interconnectedness of all life and fostering a lasting inner sense of stability and contentment with oneself. This is an unfolding and evolving process rather than an instantaneous one, but it can be greatly accelerated by cultivating a continual awareness of the true self. The best means of achieving this state is developing a routine (ideally daily) of turning inward through meditations designed to promote mindfulness and a shifting of consciousness.

Shifting Consciousness

"Shifting consciousness" always sounded like a nearly impossible skill to me, a level of mental control that only the most adept mystics could achieve, but then I learned that it is a natural process we all do every day; the trick is in learning to do it with intent. The topic of brainwaves and alpha meditation appears in my other books, and I'd like to examine it further here. The human brain operates primarily in four distinct stages: beta, alpha, theta, and delta. The beta level is when brain waves are moving between thirty to fourteen cycles per second; it is the state of normal, waking consciousness. Alpha is a bit slower, at thirteen to seven cycles per second, and this is the stage associated with meditation, relaxation, magical working, and some states of dreaming. Theta level is slower still at six to four cycles per second, and it is the state of mind associated with drowsiness, deep tranquility, psychism, and some dreaming. Delta brainwave level is the slowest state of mind with brainwaves oscillating at three cycles or less per second. Delta is the state of deep, dreamless sleep and the unconscious mind.

Essentially, when we are in normal waking consciousness our brains operate in the beta level; when we relax, mediate, or daydream, our mind slips into alpha level; when we begin to fall asleep, our brains move from alpha to theta brainwave level; and from there we slip into the deep sleep of delta. As we sleep, our brain activity alternates between the deep, dreamless sleep of delta and the accelerated mental activity of rapid eye movement (REM) sleep when brain activity picks up pace and moves back into theta. Sometimes the brain also moves into alpha level, where our subconscious mind takes the reins and we experience the world of dreams.

In practical magical application, Witches and other spell casters should learn the skill of moving from beta consciousness down into alpha (and at times even into theta) since being in these states consciously grants us access to the subconscious mind. Working all the way down into delta isn't needed in most everyday magical work as it would mean reaching the unconscious mind and a loss of self-awareness. Delta is usually only used automatically during sleep and purposefully during deep trance work or to connect to a sense of oneness and higher beings. The following exercises serve to direct the mind into the different brainwave levels. The first one, the Rainbow meditation, is a basic alpha meditation featured in *Spellcasting For Beginners*. I include it here as a starting place for any spell or psychic work and also as a springboard for the other meditations.

The Rainbow Meditation

Make yourself comfortable and close your eyes. Breathe in and out gently and evenly and see yourself outdoors, floating on a cloud. The cloud floats upward and sails toward a beautiful rainbow. The cloud takes you directly above this rainbow to the absolute peak of the rainbow's arc. At this point the cloud begins to slowly descend into the rainbow, and you find yourself surrounded by color. You begin to feel the slow descent and your field of vision is colored red. All you see is red as you pass through this part of the rainbow. Slowly, you sink deeper into the rainbow and now your vision changes and all you see is orange. The color glows and feels like being out in warm sunshine. As you drift further down through the rainbow, you move into yellow. Everything is yellow as fresh and bright as daffodils. Moving deeper into the rainbow, you now find yourself surrounded by crisp, spring green. As you continue your descent, you move into beautiful sky blue then, dark cool indigo. Your journey is almost complete as you finally sink into violet. You are now in the violet sphere of spirituality. Once you are in violet, say to yourself, "I have traveled through the spectrum and have now reached a spiritual level of power and comfort." Count down from seven to one and settle into relaxation for as long as you wish. To end this meditation, imagine yourself being drawn up quickly through the colors and out of the rainbow.

Theta Meditation

This meditation is an addition to the Rainbow meditation that will bring you down to the deeper, more relaxed theta brainwave level. After using the Rainbow meditation and becoming settled and relaxed in the violet color, visualize a small cauldron or a flower such as a rose glowing with soft blue-green light in the heart area. Since theta is a dream level of consciousness, it helps to focus on an image such as this which is slightly abstract and speaks to emotional energy; it is the heart chakra, soothing blue-green light. Hold this picture for several minutes while breathing in and out slowly and naturally.

Once this state is achieved, you can proceed with any psychic awareness exercises or auto-suggestions/affirmations directly to the subconscious mind. Working in the theta state will be examined more thoroughly in chapter 6. For now, let us move on to trying to reach the deepest state of mind—delta brainwave level.

Delta Meditation

This is the trickiest state to achieve due to the paradox it presents: once you fully reach delta level, you are unconscious and lose self-awareness. Doing this through meditation really only allows us to reach the edge, the cusp between theta and delta. We keep some level of awareness at this level, though it is really more sensation than true awareness. To begin, the rainbow meditation must be done and followed through to the theta meditation. Once you are in theta, allow the visualization of the cauldron or flower to fade. Become aware of a warm sensation in the heart area. Allow this warmth to spread throughout your entire body. Rest in this feeling of warmth for as long as desired, focusing only on this single sensation and not on any type of visualization or other stimuli. This meditation isn't really used all that often in spell casting, though it is a wonderful way to fall asleep naturally.

A couple of other useful meditations follow: the first aids in inner understanding, and the second energizes the body by activating its vital centers.

Mindfulness Meditation

A basic mindfulness meditation can be utilized in order to promote self-awareness and a more spiritually centered state of being. Mindfulness meditations are helpful to learn detached non-judgment of mind chatter and gradually, this trains the mind to become less wild and more focused and disciplined. This meditation uses the breath as a mental focus. When you are ready, with closed eyes, begin to observe your breath; don't force yourself to breathe a certain way, just observe your natural breath. Notice how your body feels as you breathe in and as you breathe out. Maintaining your focus on your breathing, also extend your awareness to your body posture and your comfort level. As you continue in passive awareness, your mind will naturally wander some. When it happens and a thought enters your mind, notice it in a detached manner and let it go. The key to this meditation is to be aware of your breathing, body, and thoughts without letting any of these things completely take over your attention. Keeping an unbiased and detached perspective during the meditation helps you develop strength of will and mental discipline while simultaneously bringing inner awareness to the forefront of consciousness. Continue this meditation for as long as desired, ideally for at least ten minutes.

Chakra Meditation

This system of energy centers within the body comes from Hindu and Buddhist traditions from Asia. In fact, the word *chakra* itself comes from the Sanskrit word for wheel. While in my own tradition we recognize three primary energy centers—the base, the heart center, and the third eye—most practitioners today recognize a total of seven primary energy centers: the base or root, navel, solar plexus, heart, throat, third eye, and crown chakras. All physically correspond to the body's major glands, and it is believed these centers are all linked together through the spinal cord. The chakras themselves are points in the etheric body through which the life force is drawn into the physical body.

Consciously focusing on these centers and activating them through meditation helps move the energy through the physical body and can help enhance our intuition, psychic awareness, and magical abilities. The base chakra relates to our ability to ground our energy into the material world. The navel chakra relates to our generative abilities both physical and psychic. The solar plexus chakra relates to our self-confidence and inner power; it is our personal nexus point where the energies of the upper and lower converge. The heart chakra relates, not surprisingly, to our emotions and our ability to give and receive love. The throat chakra relates to our ability to communicate on both a physical and spiritual level. The third eye chakra relates to our inner vision, imagination, clairvoyance, magical ability, and psychic power. Finally, the crown chakra relates to our spirituality and the ability to connect to oneness and higher beings. For this meditation, it is ideal to sit in a high backed chair to sit up straight while still being able to rest your head. Sit up straight with your feet flat on the floor and close your eyes.

To open the chakras, begin to breathe in and out slowly and naturally. When you feel comfortable, visualize energy coming up from the earth, through the floor, and into your body through the soles of your feet. Draw the energy up through your legs to your tailbone area. When it reaches this point, see the area glow with red light. Once the red glow is firmly established, visualize the energy moving up to your navel (belly button) region and see the area glow with orange light (you now have red light at the base chakra and orange light at the navel). From the navel, send the energy upward to the solar plexus region (the area of your stomach between your belly button and rib cage) and see this area glow with yellow light. From there, send the energy upward to the heart and see this area glow with green light. The energy now moves up to the base of the throat, slightly above the collar bone. Visualize this area glowing with blue light. After this, send the energy up to the third eye, the area just above the eyebrows in the middle of your forehead. See this region glowing with an indigo light. Finally, send the energy in and up so it goes through the third eye, into your brain and up to the top of your head. Visualize this area glowing with a violet light.

From this point you have two options: sending the energy out through the top of your head (this will release it to the universe), or bending it around yourself on both sides so it encircles you like an egg, through your feet once again. The first option can be used to help you to connect to the spiritual world such as when asking deities, guardians, ancestors, or guides for help or information. The second option keeps the energy personal, enlivening your chakras and protecting yourself from any unwanted energies that would interfere with your work. Whatever your choice, you can rest in this state for as long as you wish after the meditation is complete.

After practicing the chakra meditation a few times it becomes very easy to do as long as you keep the colors in their proper rainbow order and remember where the chakras are located: bottom of the spine near the tailbone, navel, solar plexus, heart, throat, third eye, and top of the head.

A daily practice of activating the chakras can be very helpful in raising psychic awareness and boosting overall health but they should not be left active all the time. You wouldn't leave a car running until there's no more gas left or abstain from sleep for forty eight hours; chakras are the same—they can become exhausted from overuse. Putting them into overdrive through meditation can help them return to normal function *if* they are blocked or it can help train them to become more powerful, but they must be brought back down to a relaxed state once the exercise is over. It is best to end the meditation by closing the chakras and sending the excess energy out of yourself.

To close the chakras and end a meditation, start with the crown chakra at the top of your head. Visualize the violet glow—almost too bright—subduing to a more normal level of brightness, and withdraw the energy down to your third eye. From there, see the indigo light fade to a normal, steady color, and send the energy back down to your throat chakra where the blue light fades. From there, send the energy down to the heart area where the green light fades and then to the solar plexus where the yellow light fades. Next, send the energy back down through the navel where the orange light fades, down to the base chakra where the red light fades back to normal. Finally, send the energy down through your legs and out through your feet, returning it to the earth. The chakras have now returned to normal, and you can open your eyes.

Developing a regular routine of using meditations to shift your consciousness, bring self-awareness, and energize your body's spiritual energy centers can be very rewarding and empowering. Once you have become more spiritually centered and train the mind to shift consciousness according to your will, you'll have a strong mental, emotional, and spiritual foundation that allows you to truly experience and appreciate the richness of life and the magic in this world; the wonders of nature surrounding us all.

THREE

Know the World

The journey of the spellcaster is a walk of wisdom. Each step brings a new lesson and life experience; all the wonderful forms of life, love, magic, and nature are ours to behold. Witch or no, we can all open ourselves to the beauty of the world and nature's intricate web. In the Craft, we are taught that the patterns and reality of the greater universe are mirrored in the reality of the immediate environment. This phenomenon of macrocosm and microcosm is repeated continually; the behavior of the solar system is mirrored by what occurs on earth (hence the study of astrology); the planet's behavior is mirrored by what happens in each individual part of the planet, and so on down the line—all the way down to our individual lives. Everything is spiritually linked and by such phenomena as air, gravity, radio waves, radiation, and so on. It is all a delicate pattern of harmony, balance, and expression summed up in

37

the maxim: as above, so below. When we strive to understand the world (and beyond); its creatures, its tides, its elements, its nature, we grow as human beings and that growth is mirrored in a growth of our magical abilities.

Connecting with Life at All Levels

Witches and other spiritual people are usually (but not always) more open to the world around them. It is such valuable training to really observe and connect with other forms of life and see similarities and differences to our own natures. Learning about other creatures and their ways not only broadens our awareness of the world, but it also gives us new insight into our own unique character. When I was younger, I noticed that my cats seemed to hug each other as they slept and my dog seemed to hug by putting his head to my shoulder. I realized how underestimated the animal kingdom truly is and that there really is no hierarchy, no "better" or "worse"—only different.

Try to spend some time outdoors even for an hour or so being fully observant—no cellphone, music, or other distractions, only the outdoors with its plants and animals. Notice the birds, ideally a large flock flying in a formation that somehow magically seems to never collide despite maneuvering in complex patterns in unison. Notice the plants: a sunflower following the path of the sun, a Venus flytrap ensnaring its prey, or a moonflower opening at night. In a city setting, grass or tree roots can usually be observed somewhere to have broken through the concrete in a powerful expression of life's determination. How can plants move without any muscle tissue? How can a tuft of grass or a tree root that we could easily cut in half be powerful enough and have the sheer strength to actually break through solid concrete? It is more important to ask questions like this than it is to find answers; keeping a sense of wonder and awe is an important part of being able to work magic. I have said before, the ability to work magic is a byproduct of spiritual training. The more we consciously choose to connect to the natural world and observe its cycles, the better we retune ourselves to the earth's rhythm. Connecting to the natural world greatly expands our ability to create change through our force of will because our will is already resonating with energy cycles of life. When we are attuned to nature, our magic is boosted like a bird flying with a tailwind.

Auras

Every living person, plant, and animal has a certain amount of electrical and spiritual energy. Some of it emanates from the physical body, making what we call the aura. Our auras are multifunctional and are in part the "organs" through which we have a psychic sense. When we "feel" someone watching us, it is the disturbance to our aura that alerts our psychic sense. Our auras act as psychic shields and as manifestations of our mood and general health. Experienced clairvoyants can see auras, and their pattern and color can even be used to diagnose illness.

Some of what we do to magically charge an object is to either give it an aura (if it is an artificial object) or "color" and shift its preexisting aura (in the case of plants, stones, and natural objects that have inherent life force) according to what we desire. We do this by implanting some of our own energy in the object's energy; we leave a piece of ourselves with the object to impart our influence. Even if we are harnessing an external energy force (e.g., channeling planetary, stellar, or divine energies, and the like), through the agency of our directed will we end up imbuing some of our essence into the magic. Magic is such a personal art, as you can see, because we literally invest our own energy into manifesting an outcome—we give life to it.

Exercise to See the Aura

To begin to see energy physically, use a healthy plant, another person as a volunteer, or hold your hand out in front of you in a dimly lit room. Place the plant, volunteer, or your outstretched hand in front of a blank wall or curtain that is a single, solid color. You can experiment with different colored backgrounds to see what works best for you.

Observe the subject. At first, it is helpful to try and observe with your peripheral vision. Eventually when your skill increases, you can begin viewing a subject directly and still see the aura. Look for any energy patterns; many times in the beginning it will look like heat waves or a light fog. Colors may not be visible at first but your ability to see them can develop over time. Sometimes it helps to move around a little while you look at the subject to see if you notice changes in the energy around the target. If you cannot see anything on the first try, don't be discouraged. Sometimes it takes weeks of practice before results are achieved. Proper development of this skill will open the door to many different types of energy work and full awareness and use of your aura. Aside from other uses of auric energy, the ability to detect the aura is a great boon for another important magical skill, transplanting of our consciousness into an external subject.

Transplanting of Consciousness

As magical practitioners, we can develop the ability to externalize our conscious awareness to the point where it can merge with the consciousness of another, including inanimate objects such as crystals or metal. This can be done to influence the subject with magical energy and give it intent or to develop a greater understanding of what it is like for the subject to exist as it does, a "walk a mile in their shoes"-type experience. Successful shapeshifting of consciousness does require some practice but it is a very interesting skill.

Before starting any training, it is helpful to understand what this skill is and what it isn't. First of all, when you shift "into" the subject you will never completely lose yourself or be unable to shift back, nor will you be "possessing" the subject or causing harm in any way. What will happen is that you'll have a type of shared awareness; the subject will still be itself, but you will also be sharing its awareness briefly, like a twin of sorts. Just as we all shift consciousness naturally through the different stages of brainwave activity, so too do we naturally transfer our conscious awareness within our own being anytime we become acutely aware of some part of our bodies. For example, when you walk into a dark room and feel around for the light switch, a large portion of your conscious awareness is transferred to your fingertips as they feel along the wall. The matter is really how much attention we are willing to devote to that awareness. Though transferring our conscious awareness to something outside ourselves is a bit more complex, the same basic principle applies.

To begin this training, it is best to use an inanimate natural object such as a crystal to make the process as easy as possible. Hold the object in your hands and consciously connect with it. Send your energy into it as if you were charging it for a spell. Once the object has been charged, set it on a table in front of you in a dimly lit room. Candlelight is good as long as candles are placed so as not to be distracting and the room is bright enough so you can clearly see the object.

Now focus your attention on the object and mentally project your consciousness out toward it, like sending energy out from your eyes into the object. After a minute or so, put your consciousness into the object. Begin to think and feel as though you were the object. As you keep your consciousness in the object, eventually you will start to notice your awareness switching back and forth between moments of thinking and feeling *like* the object and actually thinking and feeling *as* the object. With practice, you can maintain this consciousness and avoid popping out of it until you choose to on purpose. Let this be a meditative exercise. Being relaxed and at ease will help the process. Frustration or stress will only hinder the process. To return to your normal consciousness is a simple matter. All you have to do is become aware of your physical body. Focus on your breathing or think of your face, hands, or feet. Becoming aware of your physical nature draws your consciousness immediately back to yourself.

Once you have mastered this basic technique, you can use it on other objects and even animals or people, if they volunteer. To do this with animals, either have an animal with you to share its consciousness or you use the rainbow meditation to shift your consciousness into an alpha state and form a mental image of the type of animal in which you wish to shift. From there, you can merge your consciousness with this animal to identify with its nature. This skill really promotes a deep understanding of other forms of life and is the basis for other exercises such as contact with the elemental forces.

The Elements

When Witches speak of the elements, we aren't referring to the periodic table scientists have developed but rather the basic breakdown for the states of matter in our world. The original four elements of Witchcraft and western mysticism are: earth (solid), air (gas), water (liquid), and fire (heat and chemical reaction)— an understanding that goes back to at least ancient Greece. Witches recognize that the elements have spiritual counterparts; just as we have a human spirit, so too do the elements and their manifestations carry their own spirits. Witches also recognize a fifth element, that of "spirit" also known as akasha, Odic force, prana, mana, qi, and so on. Each of these words have a slightly different meaning but there is no word in English that properly sums up the fifth elemental force, so are all used to describe the energy considered the basic spiritual substance from which the other elements and all physical things form—the "God Force." Everything in existence is seen to have been manifest out of the interplay of the five elements in some combination.

I find it amusing that the system of the four elements has been decried by many people with a modern scientific mind-set since the periodic table of elements's creation. Upon close examination of the table, it is easy to see that everything in it is simply a further breakdown of the original four elements— each entry is either a solid, liquid, gas, or the result of chemical reaction. Witches recognize a spiritual side to the elements, and part of our magical training is in learning how to connect with these forces. One technique used to build this connection is known as merging, essentially another form of transferring consciousness.

To Merge with the Element of Earth

Connecting with this element helps us be grounded and centered, granting us a deeper understanding of the natural world and its inhabitants. We can also become better at summoning and healing as well. Following are two exercises to help merge with different aspects of the earth element.

CONNECT TO A TREE

Find a large tree and sit down with your back against its trunk. Close your eyes and feel the tree's solid strength as you rest against it. Breathe in and out in a relaxed manner. As you do so, visualize the energy of the tree being absorbed into your body. Breathe in and out thirteen times, each time taking in some of the tree's energy until your whole body is enveloped. Feel yourself becoming part of the tree. Call to the tree's spirit, commune with it, and settle into the feeling of being a tree. Rest in this state for as long as desired.

When you wish to return to normal, bid farewell to the tree's spirit and breathe in and out thirteen times, this time releasing the energy of the tree. Open your eyes.

Note: If for any reason you feel uncomfortable or somehow "rejected" by the tree, simply disconnect from its energy, apologize for intruding, and leave the area. It doesn't happen very often, but is a possibility.

CONNECT TO THE LAND

Find an area of land to lie upon. You can experiment with different types of ground to see how the results differ: sand, bare earth, grass, a field of wildflowers. Once you lie down, close your eyes, relax, and breathe in thirteen breaths. As you do so, absorb the land's energy. Feel your entire body filling up with the dense energy of the land as though you were becoming part of the earth itself. You can connect with the local land spirit and commune with this presence for as long as you wish. When you want to end the exercise, say goodbye to the land spirit and breathe out the earth energy before opening your eyes.

△ To Merge with the Element of Air

The air element is connected to the power of the mind; that of thought, creativity, and inspiration. Connecting to this element helps us focus, improves our clarity and memory, and can also aid our ability to connect to higher beings. Here is a simple exercise for connecting to the power of air.

CONNECT TO THE AIR

On a preferably cloudy day go outside and find a comfortable spot to sit or lie down. Gaze up at the sky and breathe in thirteen times, each time taking in the spiritual power of the air element. Relax and watch clouds for a while, connecting to the air current. Look for any shapes that form in the clouds. You can use whatever you see as an oracle, a form of scrying, or you can call to the air spirits and try to commune with them, if you wish. Eventually after enough practice, you can try to influence the shapes the clouds take. When you wish to end the exercise, thank the air spirits and breathe out the thirteen breaths of air element to return to normal.

To Merge with the Element of Water

The water element is connected to emotions, fluidity, change, and adaptability. Merging with this element brings us more in tune with our emotions and enhances our intuition. Here are two exercises for expanding our connection with water. It is possible to connect to ice or snow but since these would be uncomfortable and potentially hazardous for workings done up close, I have included only the safest options.

CONNECT TO WATER

If possible, go to a lake or pond or fill a basin or cauldron with fresh water. Sit in front of the water and breathe in thirteen breaths of its essence. Feel its coldness and fluidity. Try to sense its spiritual essence. From here you have two options: close your eyes and rest in the water's energetic power or keep your eyes open and use the water as a scrying medium. Water scrying or hydromancy is the oldest form of scrying. Connecting first to the spiritual essence before scrying can greatly enhance the art's effectiveness, particularly if you are attempting to communicate to water spirits. Softly focus your eyes on the water's surface, and notice any shapes that "appear" in the surface. To end this exercise, give thanks to the water spirit, breathe out the thirteen breaths of water energy, and return your body to normal.

CONNECT TO FALLING RAIN

When it begins to rain, go outside and allow the rain to fall on you. Breathe in thirteen breaths of the water element and close your eyes. Contemplate the rain; how the cycle of nature makes the rain possible, the evaporation and condensation, the clouds and air currents. Truly, all four elements come together for rain to be possible. Heat causes water to evaporate, the air currents cause the evaporated water to condense together into clouds, the water molecules have to form around particulate matter which is frequently small bits of microscopic dust before it is heavy enough to fall, and the rain itself falls from the sky as drops.

Notice how the rain gives a strange, clear beauty to the outdoors; bask in the experience of the falling rain. When you are ready to end the exercise, breathe out the thirteen breaths of the water element and go inside to warm up—and dry off!

To Merge with the Element of Fire

The power of fire is change. Scientifically, fire classified as a chemical reaction. It can be a volatile and expansive energy as well as warm and comforting and is indeed necessary for life to exist. Connecting to the element of fire can enliven the spirit and strengthen our force of will. When trying to merge with this element, every sensible precaution must be taken: make sure your smoke alarms are in good working order, keep water nearby, refrain from wearing flowing sleeves, keep the fire well contained, and so on.

CONNECT TO THE POWER OF FIRE

For this exercise you can choose a candle, fireplace, or a small campfire. Once the fire is lit, sit before it and gaze at the flame. Breathe in and out. As you breathe thirteen breaths, absorb some of the fire's essence. Continue to gaze at the flame and focus on its movement. Eventually, you will be able to feel the vibration, the dancing flames. Try to connect to this rhythm and call to the spirit of the fire. Commune with this energy for as long as desired. If you wish, you can scry in the flames for symbols and images from the flame spirit. When you wish to end the exercise, thank the flame spirit, breathe out the thirteen breaths of fire energy, and extinguish the fire.

Now that you've gotten to know the elements on a real, personal level, it is a good idea to contemplate what they mean to you and how you relate to their energies. The act is a powerful one—determining how we view the different powers of the elements rather than relying on the correspondences others have given us. On a piece of paper or in your magical journal, draw a large circle with an X through it so that you have four equal quadrants. Label each of the quadrants with one of the elements, and in that element's area write keywords that signify what you believe represent that element's power. A personal connection to magical correspondences can be an incredible boost to magical practice and spiritual development—it is very much worth all the time and effort.

The elements are the heart of nature. Each of these forces has its own positive and negative qualities, and each is a powerful and unique expression of the fifth element, spirit. Learning about them individually teaches a grander lesson about the harmony and balance of this planet and the universe as a whole. The four elements are truly the building blocks of life and the entire cosmos.

FOUR

Know the Heavens

As the earth circles around the sun, the star that is the heart of our solar system, it is held in its elliptical path by gravitational force, as are all the other planets orbiting our sun. As we circle the sun, so too does the moon orbit around earth, also held in place through earth's gravitational force, a power that is one of our direct links to the influence of these heavenly bodies. Each component of our solar system has a different sphere of influence; the interplay of aspects and energies radiate down and affect life on earth—and in some cases, the course of our individual lives.

Though my main focus is on magical information regarding the influences of the celestial bodies and the roles their energies can play in our spells and rituals, information regarding the zodiac and how the field of astrology can bring new insight into both our magic and our lives is also included. The first celestial object covered is arguably the most important. It is a power source, a marker of time, a focus of adoration and awe, a physical symbol of divine energy made manifest, and an oracle through which important omens can be revealed—it is the moon.

☽ The Moon

The bright orb of glowing silver-white light with its continual progression through each phase, earth's only natural satellite has captured the imagination of artists, philosophers, writers, and poets for countless generations. The moon has also been a vital element of Witches' magic both in the popular mind and in practice for untold centuries.

The moon offers us its light, gravity, and power not only as the source of lunar energy but also as a conduit to the other cosmic energies in our solar system. Many people, from various astrologers to ceremonial magicians such as Henry Cornelius Agrippa, have written that the moon is a key to the influence of all the other planets in the solar system. Astrologers speak of the planetary aspects as influencing the trends of our lives while ceremonial magicians refer to drawing in magical energy for use in amplifying their own ability to create influence, but it is essentially the same principle either way.

The moon is ever-changing in its orbit around the earth; it has the swiftest movement through the zodiac and thus creates many aspects to the other planets (astrologically speaking, the word "planet" is also used to describe the sun and moon).

These aspects create a pathway for the energy of the planet to reach the moon and in turn, be channeled down to us. More information on astrology appears later in this chapter.

I remember this concept seemed terribly complicated to me when I was first taught it, but in essence it means that part of timing our magical workings can include a glance at an astrology guide to see if the moon is in harmony with any planetary forces we would like to draw upon in our spell. If, for example, we are working for good luck, it is best to cast the spell when the moon is both in a waxing phase and also in a harmonious aspect to the planet Jupiter. The energy of Jupiter is aligned with growth, expansion, luck, and influence—to be able to draw upon it and channel it into our intention is a huge boon to our magical endeavors.

The moon is an essential part of a Witch's (and realistically, anyone else's) magic. The moon is a primary energy source as well as a key indicator of when to act magically speaking and in life generally. The moon begins in darkness; the zero point of the dark/new moon. This point of stillness is the culmination of the waning cycle and gives us a point to catch our breath and take a clear look at things and see what, if anything, we would like to change. In my tradition, it is customary to settle any problems or family grievances at this time as well as give thanks for blessings and plan a working for the next full moon. Generally speaking, the "dark moon" refers to when the moon is not visible in the sky at all, and a "new moon" refers to the day or two after when the moon first becomes visible during the sunset. The dark moon gives rise to the new crescent moon. This is the time that truly begins the moon's waxing cycle. As it grows in strength and light and we are swept up in its gravitational influence, we can harness the increasing energy to work magic that initiates positive change.

When the moon is full, it is in exact opposition to the sun and the gravity—more specifically, the "tidal effect"—of the sun and the moon are in relatively similar proportion, pulling at the earth from opposite directions. Though large, the sun is approximately 391 times further away from the earth as the moon. Just as the earth is held in orbit around the sun, we hold the moon in our orbit. Gravity's force is less intense the further the distance between the objects. Though the sun has the gravitational power to hold us in orbit, its tidal effect is actually less intense than the tidal effect of the moon. This is due to the way the gravitational force spreads out across the earth and how close the moon is to us versus how far away the planet is from the sun. Simply speaking, the earth is small and far away, so the tidal effect of the sun ends up being only 44 percent as strong as the tidal pull from the moon since the moon is much closer.[1] During a full moon, we stand in the middle of the gravitational interplay and—possibly because we are predominantly watery creatures—this lunar phase opens up our psychic centers and creates an atmosphere conducive to both the magic of spell work and the magic of spiritual

---

1 "Tidal Influences," in Hyperphysics hosted by Georgia State University
   http://hyperphysics.phy-astr.gsu.edu/hbase/tide.html#mstid.

communion. The gravitational pull activates our potential, and we can harness the lunar energy which carries with it the power of the cosmos as a result. This magical force is transmitted to the earth through the moonlight which (aside from the gravitational thing) is the main reason that magic performed during the full moon is so effective. This is the time when the moon emits the peak amount of lunar and cosmic energies.

After the full moon, light decreases and wanes to the dark moon once again. The energy and light gradually diminish during the waning phase, and thus our personal energies and the earth's natural energy are much more the dominant focus at this time. This is why the phase of the waning moon is an ideal time for introspection, study, meditation, self-assessment, release, banishment, and dissolution; we are much more tuned in to our personal energy and the earth's grounding nature so that magic involving turning inward or casting away is more easily used. *Magic works best when we ride on the current of the prevailing energies.* If we work against the tide, it is still possible to achieve a goal, but it is needlessly difficult; such hard work should be reserved for emergency situations so we do not exhaust ourselves. Sometimes we have to be like the salmon and swim upstream…but it's not an everyday activity! The dominant themes of the waning moon are contraction, diminishment, and a turning-inward perspective culminating in the "rebirth" of the dark/new moon when the cycle begins again.

The moon is considered feminine in its polarity. The colors associated with the lunar energy are silver and light gray.

The metal relating to the moon is silver. Gemstones linked to the moon include moonstone and selenite. The day of the week ruled by the moon is Monday. A short list of plants ruled by the moon include: willow, moonwort, grape, mushrooms, and camphor.

The Sun

While the energy of the moon is ever-changing, altered and influenced by its waxing and waning and rapid shifting through the zodiac, the sun's energy is significantly steadier in its flow. In our orbit around it, the sun appears (to us) to travel through the twelve signs of the zodiac from one sign to the next roughly every thirty days. The movement is much slower than the moon's glide, which happens every two or three days. And because it is slower, solar energy is more dominant but less direct in its power. The sun's influence is seen in its journey through the astrological signs, as each sign expresses a different energy and focus. For the duration the sun passes through an individual sign, the solar energy is channeled into its sphere of influence. As the sun makes its way through a sign, the very nature and quality of people and animals born in that brief window are swayed by the prevailing energies. People born during the sun's pass through Leo, for example, almost invariably carry certain similar personality traits that identify them as Leos even though their individual astrological data may vary. The placement of the sun during a person's birth reveals qualities of personality, ego, and spirit; how a person relates to the world.

The sun is considered masculine in its polarity. The colors associated with solar energies are yellow, light orange, and gold. The metal that relates to the sun is gold. Gemstones linked to the sun include citrine, sunstone, and topaz. The day of the week ruled by the sun is (of course) Sunday. A short list of herbs ruled by the sun include: chamomile, cinnamon, rosemary, and sunflower.

The sun is an energizer; it is a projector of not only heat and light but of full spectrum raw energy. It carries within it the entire rainbow of possibility which is why it can be channeled to empower any type of character or intention. The rest of the heavenly bodies in our solar system are more focused in their qualities, by contrast. Each planet has a vibrational rate that resonates with specific traits and intentions; their energy can be harnessed for our magical use.

The Planets and Their Influence

Each of the planets—Mercury, Venus, Mars, Jupiter, Saturn, Uranus, Neptune, and our lil' dwarf planet, Pluto—each reflect the light of the sun and emit powerful energy fields in their own right. This used to be considered merely a symbolic magical notion but in fact it is a scientific reality. Astronomic observations though satellites and radio telescopes tells us that each planet emits varying forms of infrared light and thermal radiation due in part to gravitational pressure, atmospheric conditions, and/or leftover heat from the formation of the planet itself. It has been observed that the planets are emitting more energy than they are receiving from the sun which disproves the belief (that many people still hold) that only stars emit energy and that planets merely reflect energy from starlight.

Because planetary energies are emitted as various forms of light energy, it travels in all directions, moving very swiftly. Light travels at approximately 186,282 miles per second, which basically means that if planetary light energy is being emitted by Pluto at its distance from Earth, 4.6 billion miles (7.5 billion kilometers) away, then the energy will reach earth within seven hours.

There is a continual output of energy from each planet in the solar system reaching earth 24 hours a day, and it can be called upon and used in our magic to boost our own ability to manifest intention. If we are calling in the energy of Pluto, we do not have to wait for seven hours for it to arrive (which is pretty fast), there is already energy from Pluto in the immediate area waiting to be accessed. As we are working within our solar system, we would never have to wait longer than about seven hours for the energy of any planet to reach earth; every other celestial body in the solar system is closer than Pluto and its seven-hour journey. As such, planetary energy can reach us very quickly. The importance lies in when we wish to harness the multi-layered web of energy created when planets form an astrological aspect. When an aspect is formed, the energy emitted from the planets involved reaches earth in that same pattern and can be called upon to manifest that aspect's meaning. It can get complicated; each planet has individual qualities and the zodiac has many constellations and houses, but with time and practice it can become a powerful method of magic.

To begin, let us look at the individual planets and see their spiritual qualities and how we may draw in their energies for our use.

☿ *Mercury*

The fastest planet in the solar system, it only takes 88 days for Mercury to orbit the sun. Much like the deity for which it was named, it is considered a great messenger of the planets. Having Mercury in any aspect to another planet helps convey that planet's message more accurately. In magical terms, if Mercury is aligned with a planet whose energies we are trying to tap, it will act as a magical booster to clarify our intent. Mercury rules intelligence, communication, interpretation, teaching and studying, the written word, contracts, modes of travel, commerce, and bartering. The energy of Mercury can be called on to aid a magical intention related to any of those areas of influence. Conversely, when Mercury is poorly aspected or in one of its infamous retrogrades, all of these areas have stressed energy that can become quite chaotic.

A retrograde is when a planet appears to be moving backward in its orbit from our vantage point. The planet Mercury experiences it about three times per year. Every planet in the solar system appears to go retrograde at one point or another, due to the fact we move significantly faster than the outer planets around the sun. When we pass by them, they appear to be moving backward. Our inner planets, Mercury and Venus, go retrograde due to the opposite effect; their orbit is much swifter than ours. Because they are so close to the sun, they appear to move backward when they pass ahead of us.

The trick to dealing with a Mercury retrograde period in particular is moving backward, like the planet itself. Mercury retrograde is all about "re" activities: re-thinking, re-doing, re-evaluating, re-turning, re-viewing, re-membering, re-assessing, and so on. To navigate the retrograde with ease, entirely new projects should be avoided, but anything involving a "re-" is not only safe but can actually be wondrously successful at this time. For example, shopping—especially for anything electronic—is usually highly discouraged during a retrograde, but I have had some of my best shopping ever during Mercury retrogrades when seeking to *re*-place something that was worn out or broken. As long as what I bought wasn't something entirely new and the item was a true replacement of something (as in, a TV to replace a broken one as opposed to an additional TV), I could buy electronics without a problem.

Admittedly, it does sound a bit paranoid to those who are unfamiliar with the nature of Mercury retrogrades to be so intensely cautious and adhere to such oddly specific rules, but once I noticed the pattern of events that unfold during these times of flux, it became much easier and more practical to ride the prevailing wave of energy rather than trying to fight it and deal with the consequences.

The colors associated with the planetary energies of Mercury are orange and gray. The metals that relate to the planet are aluminum and quicksilver (mercury). Gemstones linked to Mercury include carnelian, agate, and amethyst. The day of the week ruled by Mercury is Wednesday. A short list of herbs ruled by Mercury include: cinquefoil, dill, fennel, lavender, and marjoram.

♀ Venus

The next planet, like the goddess for which she was named, governs the areas of love, friendship, and beauty. Venus's orbit around the sun takes approximately 225 days, and its orbit is near circular, unlike the rest of the planets which have an elliptical orbit. Venus is special, as it shares similar traits with Earth: they are nearly identical in diameter, mass, and density. There are many differences, of course; on Earth we don't have to worry about sulfuric gas clouds in our atmosphere, also a day (a full rotation) on Venus would last approximately 243 hours compared to our 24, and a year (a completion of one orbit) is 225 days long—that is, a day on Venus is longer than a year! Compared to the rotation of the other planets in our solar system, Venus spins backward. And speaking of backward motion, Venus goes retrograde on average about once every twenty months. During a Venus retrograde period, old friends or lovers may resurface in our lives but financial affairs may be lessened or delayed. Additionally, it is highly discouraged to buy luxury items or anything art-related during a Venus retrograde since these items fall under this planets sphere of influence. A Venus retrograde lasts approximately forty days.

Magically and astrologically speaking, Venus rules over not only love, beauty, and friendship, but also joy, harmony, luxury, self-esteem, femininity, fertility, glamour, and gifts. Perhaps surprisingly, Venus also has a very strong influence over financial gain and money matters. It might seem strange to call upon the energy of Venus in a money spell but doing so adds substantial benefit.

The colors associated with the planetary energies of Venus are pink, green, and copper. The metal that relates to the planet is copper. Gemstones linked to Venus include: malachite, emerald, and rose quartz. The day of the week ruled by Venus is Friday. A short list of herbs ruled by Venus include: apple, rose, spearmint, thyme, and yarrow.

Mars

Called the red planet, the redness of Mars occurs due to high concentrations of iron oxide in its soil. Mars is only about half the size of the Earth and has an orbit about twice as long as ours; a Martian year is about two of our years. Because the planet's orbit is longer than earth's, Mars goes retrograde only about once every 26 months but it lasts longer than a Mercury or Venus retrograde, roughly between two and three months. During a Mars retrograde, one is advised to avoid starting new projects. This time period is much more suited to reevaluating existing endeavors and determining where one can best direct time and energy.

Mars is the "warrior planet" known for strength, courage, assertiveness, power, force, action, passion, athletics, competition, risk-taking, war, combat, and masculine energy. A magical working with an intention relating to any of the above qualities is powerfully enhanced by calling upon the energy of Mars. The color associated with the planetary energy of Mars is red. The metals relating to the planet are iron and steel. Gemstones linked to Mars include: ruby, garnet, hematite, and jasper. The day of the week ruled by Mars is Tuesday. A short list of herbs ruled by Mars include: chili peppers, nettle, garlic, ginger, and pine.

Jupiter

The planet Jupiter is the largest in our solar system, larger than all of the other planets in our solar system combined! Called "the Great Benefic" by astrologers, Jupiter is considered to be the bringer of luck and opportunity wherever its influence falls. Jupiter has the largest magnetic field of any planet in the solar system. Additionally it has the strongest energy output of all the planets, regularly emitting more energy than it receives from the sun. This is the planetary energy that can be called upon in magic.

The magical intentions governed by Jupiter include such areas as luck, expansion, success, influence of people in authority, law, business, new opportunities, long-range vision, wealth (especially when combined with Venus), hope, faith, optimism and honesty. When Jupiter is retrograde, which occurs approximately every 13 months for about 4 months at a time, its energy is reversed or flipped and what was outward expansion, transforms to introspection. It is a time for inner growth and delving into the more spiritual aspects of life. Astrologically speaking, Jupiter is never considered fully negative or adversarial in nature no matter the aspect and in retrograde this planet's power lies in guiding us to inner truth and integrity. Jupiter in retrograde can be very beneficial for all forms of healing. Unlike a Mercury retrograde in which it is advised to delay any contract or business related matters if possible, projects we have already been working on can be continued without issue during Jupiter's journey backward; the only caution being against starting any brand new endeavor unless it is tied in some way to the past.

The colors associated with the planetary energy of Jupiter are blue (particularly royal blue) and purple. The metals related to the planet are tin and pewter. Gemstones linked to Jupiter include: blue sapphire, lapis lazuli, turquoise, and amethyst. The day of the week ruled by Jupiter is Thursday. A short list of herbs ruled by Jupiter include: anise, cloves, nutmeg, and sage.

♄ Saturn

Ah, Saturn; taskmaster and timekeeper. This planet that marks our transition from youthful exploits to full on (some would say unrelenting) adulthood. While beautiful with its many rings, the planet has a bit of an unsavory reputation. Saturn is the second largest planet in the solar system in terms of mass but has the lightest density, composed mostly of swirling gasses with a core of very condensed metallic hydrogen that gives the planet its innate magnetic field. Saturn orbits the sun almost twenty-nine-and-a-half years for a full revolution. Named after the Roman god who is essentially Father Time, this planet's energy relates to ambition, productivity, tangible effort and reward, concentration, aging, responsibility, authority, constriction, delay, rules, *discipline* (*the* most important quality under its domain), fear, denial, control (distinct from discipline), binding, banishing and/or neutralizing evil, and separation. As unpleasant as much of that may sound, Saturn presides over genuine progress. Saturn's type of influential energy is the type that creates and maintains form out of chaos. It is a very important energy that brings about the tangible result of the expansion capabilities of Jupiter, for example. Saturn tempers all that is unrealistic or excessive and hones the potential into actuality; it is true manifestation.

Wherever Saturn lies in our astrological chart when we are born, it will take roughly twenty-nine years for it to return to that same position. This time period, somewhere between our twenty-eighth and thirtieth birthdays, is known as our Saturn Return. During this time, a person invariably experiences a life shift that causes one to "grow up" and reach greater maturity. This time is seen as emergence into true adulthood, a transition from youth to adult/parent. A second Saturn return occurs around our fifty-eighth birthday and (astrologically) marks one's emergence into crone or sage-hood. A third return occurs around age eighty-seven, marking entry into our ancient wise one stage of life. Some of these transitions can be traumatic, but they ultimately lead us to greater wisdom, maturity, and our true selves.

In and of itself, a return isn't bad; I met my true love during my Saturn return, and the experience definitely caused me to grow and mature as a person. Blending our lives together was a process that lent itself to many important lessons and adaptations (we're the same age so we were both going through our returns when we met) on both our parts which has created and maintained an inseparable bond. I also began seriously writing during my Saturn return. Most of my life, I wrote little, creative-writing kinds of things, but it wasn't until the return that I was able to truly find my voice as a writer and move forward in a concrete fashion. It is said that as we age, we have less trouble with Saturn's energy as it rules aging and maturity, so each successive return is smoother.

Though Saturn Returns are rare occurrences during a lifetime, Saturn retrogrades annually, lasting for about four and a half months. Normally, Saturn is the teacher/parent authoritative in style, tough but fair. When the planet goes retrograde, it is harsher in its approach. We pay the price for any mistakes we have made or lessons we have failed to learn. This is the planet of self-discipline and responsibility. If we have been lacking in these areas, we will be led to confront the problem during a retrograde. That is, greater responsibilities will be heaped upon us or greater temptation will arise, and if we give in and fail to learn our lesson, things will go awry. It is best to avoid reckless behavior during a Saturn retrograde; skydiving, mountain climbing, or any other thrill-seeking activities are not advisable.

The colors associated with the planetary energy of Saturn are burgundy and magenta. The metal that relates to the planet is lead. Gemstones linked to Saturn include: black onyx, jet, coal, and diamond. The day of the week ruled by Saturn is Saturday. A short list of herbs ruled by Saturn include: black cherry, ivy, hemlock, mandrake, tobacco, wolfsbane, and plum.

Uranus

"Zany" is the word that comes to mind when trying to think of a way to describe this planet. Like Venus, Uranus spins clockwise in its rotation but unlike Venus, also spins on its side! It also has a warped, wobbly orbit around the sun, shifting from the sun appearing directly over one pole to directly over the other every forty-two of our years. Perhaps due to its odd behavior, Uranus is seen to rule over the areas of creativity, innovation, technology, surprise, electricity, genius, madness, humanitarianism, environmentalism, social change, and experimentation.

Though the epitome of non-conformity, Uranus is also scientific, rational, and a seeker of truth. Mercury is linked to this planet, as both are related to the power of the mind. Mercury is the "lower octave" related to everyday thinking, communication, and perception; Uranus is the "higher octave," related to abstract or intuitive thinking, flashes of inspiration, genius, and wisdom gained from experience. Where Saturn transforms effort and ideas into concrete reality, Uranus elaborates on this action to customize and integrate new concepts into existing reality, expanding knowledge and potential. Uranus seeks truth and individuality. It is said that while Saturn rules aging, Uranus rules youth. It's not surprising—the effects of this planet are often sudden and unexpected, exemplifying the impetuous nature and exuberance of youth.

Despite this planet's lightning bolt-type nature, Uranus has a very slow orbit around the sun, roughly eighty-four years. Its slow orbit means that those flashes of change and advancement come primarily on a broad, societal level versus the narrow, personal level as is the style of Mercury. When Uranus goes retrograde, its usual revolutionary nature turns a bit more aggressive. Uranus in direct motion is more attuned to nonviolent protests and picketing whereas Uranus in retrograde is the energy of rioting and political upheaval. Any issues seem much more magnified during a retrograde, and anything that has been pushed to the side or swept under the rug pops out, demanding attention and resolution. Retrogrades tend to push us as individuals and on the societal level into reevaluating thoughts, actions, and behaviors to strip away anything false, forced, or no longer relevant so we may continue to improve as living beings. On the plus side, our intuition tends to be more accurate during a Uranus retrograde. Uranus spends about half of the year in retrograde; despite its qualities of change and rebellion, its effects are not always drastic or chaotic.

The colors associated with the planetary energy of Uranus are lavender and bright white. The metals relating to the planet are uranium and white gold. Gemstones linked to Uranus include: clear quartz, rutilated quartz, and fire opal. A short list of herbs ruled by Uranus include: rue, guarana, pomegranate, and peppermint.

♆ *Neptune*

This planet was discovered in the mid-1800s and is said to preside over the areas of self-sacrifice, altruism, romanticism, dreams, belief, compassion, kindness, and spirituality. Neptune rules over all things psychic, intuitive, clairvoyant, abstract, and artful. Neptune is a large planet with a nearly 165 year orbit, so its influence is broad in its reach. It takes approximately fourteen years to move from one sign to another, so its influence is on a generational level. The best example is Neptune in Scorpio which was from 1957 to 1971, fully encompassing the decade of the 1960s, a time of societal change; civil rights, anti-war, hippie, feminist, and gay rights movements gathered serious momentum during this period. Scorpio rules breaking through limits, and Neptune in Scorpio shifts the energy to the peak of limitless idealism, the hallmark of the 1960s (more about this in the zodiac section). Neptune is linked to Venus, as they are both attuned to the energy of love. Venus is the lower octave of personal feeling, and Neptune is the higher octave of transcendent, selfless love.

Neptune turns retrograde for about half of the year like Uranus, and the dreams, intuitive feelings, and deeply felt ideals are more able to manifest in the world. The potentially troublesome qualities of a Neptune retrograde are the burgeoning psychic and emotional energies that surface—these can be difficult influences for those of us who are empathic. Difficult relationships or emotional issues that have been left to fester in the background will demand more attention in an attempt for resolution. The key to navigating a retrograde with greater ease is to realize that we are more driven toward action during this time and must be consciously aware of which actions to take and to ignore for now. We needn't be slaves to the patterns of energy; we have the free will to outmaneuver most of the impulses brought on by these planetary shifts.

The colors associated with the planetary energy of Neptune are all glowing, iridescent, or opalescent colors and swirls of white, light blue, and lavender. The metal related to the planet is platinum. Gemstones linked to Neptune include: aquamarine, bloodstone, and opals. A short list of herbs ruled by Neptune include: coffee, lotus, poppy, and seaweeds.

Pluto

Named in honor of the Roman Lord of the Underworld, this planet's nature is that of a phoenix rising from the ashes, a powerful catalyst for irrevocable transformation, and the great destructor. Discovered in 1930, it is the furthest known planet from the sun in our system. Pluto is now officially classified as a "dwarf planet" (only half the size of Mercury and actually smaller than our moon) but its influence should never be underestimated. It takes almost 250 years for Pluto to fully circle the sun. Pluto can stay in a single astrological sign anywhere from thirteen to twenty-five years, so most people in the same generation have a similar Pluto placement in their astrological birth chart.

Pluto rules over large-scale change whether to unite or disrupt; transformations of any kind, upheavals, death, rebirth, psychology (particularly in relation to obsessions), sexuality, insurance, debt, taxes, loans, inheritance, mutation, waste, and elimination. The energy of Pluto should be used with caution: it most certainly cannot be entirely controlled. Pluto possesses enormous power and a relentless energy that if needed can manifest seemingly impossible change, but there is always a cost. I personally don't consider Pluto as evil, but approaching any dealings with the planet as give-and-take or a Faustian deal rather than an easy partnership is wise when working with its energy. Where Neptune is selfless, Pluto demands recompense for its efforts. In my experience, this usually involves having very precise terms for your magic, leaving no room for interpretation and knowing and accepting that there will be aspects of the manifestation that will be unforeseen, uncomfortable, and beyond control; this is Pluto's price, and it forces us to grow spiritually. My best advice is to work with Pluto only when critically necessary; trivial matters don't mesh well with this energy—like using a fire hose to put out a candle.

The positive side to Pluto is that its transformative abilities encourage new growth and evolution. Its investigative nature greatly aids uncovering hidden truth and the inner workings of things. Pluto is linked to Mars in its nature; Pluto is the higher octave and Mars the lower. Mars is a warrior/conqueror and Pluto is the conqueror/rebuilder. Pluto always has a phoenix aspect to it; it destroys but does so with a purpose, to build anew. Pluto goes into retrograde for about half of each year and when this planet goes retrograde; its energy is not diminished but rather more concentrated. Pluto in retrograde channels our energy more toward confronting inner conflicts rather than Pluto in regular, direct motion which calls on us to channel our energies outward. The intensity of Pluto can be more overwhelming during a retrograde cycle since it is directed inward, so it is a good idea to do more grounding meditations during this cycle.

The color associated with the planetary energy of Pluto is black. The metals related to the planet are chrome, plutonium, and all other radioactive elements. Gemstones linked to Pluto include: obsidian, black coral, and black aventurine. A short list of herbs ruled by Pluto include: black cohosh, blue cohosh, and wormseed.

 ### The Zodiac

From our vantage point on earth, the sky appears to circle around us in a glorious blanket of stars. Through the (near) center of the sky is a belt of constellations known as the zodiac through which the sun, moon, and all the planets appear to pass in their orbit. Though the constellations aren't exactly equidistant from each other, the zodiac itself has been divided into twelve equal portions, one for each constellation. Together these make up the twelve signs of astrology, and the signs are divided into the four physical elements: earth, air, fire, and water. They are also portioned into three qualities: cardinal, fixed, and mutable.

Earth signs are considered to be the most grounded and logical in nature, air signs the most social and communicative, water signs the most nurturing and emotional, and the fire signs the most independent and spontaneous. Regarding the qualities, cardinal signs begin a season and are the initiators, the bringers of change. The fixed signs are in the middle of each season. They personify the season and are usually the most stubborn signs; they resist change but have the most resilience and perseverance. Mutable signs are last, and they signify a shift into a new season. Their energy helps to release the energy of the old season and prepare for the new. Mutable signs are the most adaptable, flexible, and visionary when it comes to intellectual concepts.

The divisions of the zodiac are not only made up of the signs. Underlying and accompanying the signs are "houses," twelve numbered sections corresponding to an individual's astrological chart. When an astrologer casts a birth chart showing a client's planetary placements at the time of their birth, each sign is designated by a house number to illustrate how the various signs and planetary aspects affect the person individually. A person's sun sign always becomes the sign of the first house in a solar chart. A person's rising sign—the sign that on the eastern horizon at the exact time of birth—can also be called their first house, but that is not particularly relevant to this discussion. Because not everyone is born an Aries (the original first sign), our personal charts are adjusted so that our sun sign is always in the first house of our solar chart. For an Aries-born person, the sign number and house number match, for the rest of us there is variance. Using myself as an example, I am a Leo; for me Leo is my first house in my solar chart, Virgo is the second house, and so on around the zodiac.

Each house is said to reflect how a person expresses a sign's energy in life. Houses not only have traditional individual meanings but also collective meaning based on their element and where they occur in the chart. Beyond their individual number, there are three classifications for houses: angular, succedent, and cadent. These designations share kinship with the three qualities of cardinal, fixed, and mutable.

Angular houses: The first, fourth, seventh, and tenth describe the person, their opposite, their foundation, and their ambitions. These are the houses of action.

Succedent houses: The second, fifth, eighth, and eleventh describe what a person has, loves, obstacles and debts, and friends and associates.

Cadent houses: The third, sixth, ninth, and twelfth describe how a person communicates; work and health; learning, philosophy, and secrets; and sacrifice and selflessness.

Looking at things from an elemental standpoint, the houses keep their elemental designation regardless of whatever sign occupying them in a chart. For example: a person could have Gemini in their first house but the first house is still a fire house elementally speaking, even though Gemini itself is an air sign.

Fire houses: The first, fifth, and ninth houses are considered the "trinity of life." They relate to a person's attitude, confidence, and faith.

Earth houses: The second, sixth, and tenth houses are considered the "trinity of wealth." They relate to a person's level of practicality; how essential needs are met and resources managed, and how a person relates to the physical world and personal achievements.

Air houses: The third, seventh, and eleventh houses are considered the "trinity of relationships." They relate to how a person communicates, collaborates, and socializes.

Water houses: The fourth, eighth, and twelfth houses are considered "the psychic trinity." They relate to a person's emotional foundation, coping with adversity, and fulfilling personal needs.

In general, the way I was taught to remember the areas high-lighted by the houses was the following simplified list:

- I
- have
- communication
- home
- love
- work
- partnerships
- obstacles
- learning
- career
- friendship
- secrets

When the sun, moon, or a planet travels through an astrological sign, inherent energy is channeled into expression through the sign's particular style of communication. For example, the energy of the sun in Aries (the beginning of spring) is felt much differently than the energy of the sun in Aquarius (the middle of winter). Sometimes, a planet's energy is not very compatible with the energy of the sign through which it is passing, and other times the energy is fantastically compatible. Four areas describe the relationship of the signs with the planets. These are known as dignity, detriment, exaltation, and fall.

Dignity: Each astrological sign is said to be ruled by at least one planet. When a planet is traveling through the sign it rules, the planet is said to be in its dignity, the placement in which the planet's energy is expressed in its strongest, most natural form. The planet and the sign they rule are listed as follows:

Sun–Leo, Mercury–Gemini and Virgo, Venus–Taurus and Libra, Moon–Cancer, Mars–Aries and (partially) Scorpio, Jupiter–Sagittarius and (partially) Pisces, Saturn–Capricorn and (partially) Aquarius, Uranus–Aquarius, Neptune–Pisces, Pluto–Scorpio.

The reason Mars, Jupiter, and Saturn have partial rulership over Scorpio, Pisces, and Aquarius is that these planets were considered to be the only rulers of those signs before the later planets—Uranus, Neptune, and Pluto—were known to exist. Once these planets were discovered and their attributes determined, they were given rulership over their signs. However, the original rulers are still considered by many to have a secondary influence over those signs. Though an ancient practice, astrology is very progressive. When new discoveries are made, they are incorporated into the greater system.

Detriment: The detriment of a planet is easy to find. It is the opposite sign from the ruling sign. Some astrologers call the detriment placement the "debilitation" instead. As some planets rule two signs, there are two detriment signs as well. When a planet is traveling through its detriment sign, it is considered to be at a general disadvantage. The moon, for example, is not as able to express its full emotional nature in reserved Capricorn, its detriment. This isn't necessarily a "bad" placement, especially since having a strong ability to keep emotions in check can be considered a positive quality; a moon in Capricorn is a more cool and detached moon (more later in this chapter). As it relates to magic, the supposed disadvantage of the detriment placement turns into a strong magical advantage when you wish to use the planet's energy to communicate with someone of the sign in question or when working for a goal that falls under the influence of that sign. Using the same example, the moon in Capricorn is an excellent position to communicate on an emotional level with a Capricorn person or to use magic for material achievement through logical application of emotional concepts. Political advertising and debate are well suited to this placement, as is negotiating with superiors or other important people in relation to career matters. The same is true for other planets in their detriments. There is always a way to turn a disadvantage into an advantage using the energy along its preferred path. The planets and their sign(s) of detriment are as follows:

Sun–Aquarius, Mercury–Sagittarius and Pisces, Venus–Scorpio and Aries, Moon–Capricorn, Mars–Libra and (partially) Taurus, Jupiter–Gemini and (partially) Virgo, Saturn–Cancer and (partially) Leo, Uranus–Leo, Neptune–Virgo, Pluto–Taurus.

Exaltation: When a planet is in exaltation, it is said to be in the sign in which it is the most able to fully express its highest potential, in some ways even more than in the sign it rules. This isn't to say that this is a more "powerful" placement than a ruling sign necessarily, only that in exaltation a planet's influence is channeled to the most positive end of the spectrum. An example would be Venus in Pisces, expressing the loving character of Venus in a transcendent manner, fully focusing on the sensitive and selfless aspects of love, art, and beauty. Venus in Libra (its planetary ruler, is powerful but runs the risk of being flighty and aloof at times. Venus in Taurus, also a powerful ruling placement, can at times become selfish and materialistic. The only problem for a planet in exaltation is that it may become too much of itself. In the Pisces example, Venus could become too eager to self-sacrifice, forgetting—or outright refusing—to take care of the self in favor of over-nurturing another. Magically speaking, when a planet is in exaltation, its energy can be channeled for the highest good of its nature. When you want pure, positive planetary energy, exaltation is the time to work. The planets and their signs of exaltation are listed here:

Sun–Aries, Mercury–Virgo, Venus–Pisces, Moon–
Taurus, Mars–Capricorn, Jupiter–Cancer, Saturn–Libra,
Uranus–Scorpio, Neptune–Gemini, Pluto–Leo

It is worth mentioning that the generally accepted
exaltation sign for Mercury is Virgo, a sign also ruled by
Mercury. This is the only instance in which a ruling sign
and a sign of exaltation coincide. Some astrologers believe
Aquarius is the sign of exaltation for Mercury since
Aquarius is ruled by Uranus and Uranus is considered
the higher octave of Mercury, but my feeling is that
because Aquarius is a fixed sign, its nature is not as
harmonious for the fullest expression of Mercury's
energy as mutable Virgo.

Fall: Opposite of a planet's sign of exaltation is the
sign of a planet's "fall." Much like the detriment,
this placement is considered to be somewhat of a
disadvantage. Since exaltation is the placement of a
planet's purest expression, the fall is the placement
of the least comfortable expression. An example is
Mercury, whose exaltation as previously noted is Virgo.
Mercury is perfectly comfortable in this analytical and
detail oriented sign, but in Pisces, the sign of Mercury's
fall, the sharp mental processes and critical nature of
Mercury is curtailed and is turned more toward artistic
pursuits and has an uncharacteristic forgetful streak
and lack of structure that would be unthinkable to

Mercury in Virgo. On the other hand, Mercury in Pisces can be very intuitive and much more attuned to the subconscious and psychic mind than any other Mercury placement. And that's the secret of the fall—it is not really bad or a disadvantage, rather the yin, the necessary and opposite expression counter to the yang of the exaltation. In practical magical application, when a planet is in its fall, it is an ideal time to work for the polar opposite of the planet's active nature. So Mercury in Pisces is an excellent time for psychic work whereas Mercury in Virgo would be much more appropriate for studying, writing, and communication. The planets and their signs of fall are as follows:

Sun–Libra, Mercury–Pisces, Venus–Virgo, Moon–Scorpio, Mars–Cancer, Jupiter–Capricorn, Saturn–Aries, Uranus–Taurus, Neptune–Sagittarius, Pluto–Aquarius.

Understanding and following each astrological sign and/or house, how the energy of each planet is altered while passing through a sign, and how to harness their innate correspondence magically is key. Most of us know our own sun sign and maybe a bit about other signs as far as personality traits are concerned, but there is so much more. Astrology deals with cosmic energies channeled to the earth, so gaining knowledge and proper use of these planetary forces is a very valuable enhancement for our magic.

Though the new year begins on January 1 according to the Gregorian calendar, October 31 is the generally accepted start of the Witches' new year. The astrological year begins at the vernal equinox with the sun's transit into Aries.

Aries

Aries is the first sign of the zodiac. The sun moves into this sign on the first day of spring around March 21 and moves through it until about April 19 or 20. As initiator of spring in the northern hemisphere, it is a cardinal sign. Because spring is the time of greatest growth, Aries is considered the most energetic of the cardinal signs, possessing an enormous reserve of pure strength, energy, and willpower especially suited to new beginnings, ideas, and uncharted approaches. A fire sign, Aries has enormous drive and determination. Its symbol is the ram, an animal known for its stubborn streak and ability to climb to the highest peaks. Aries are very equipped to handle challenges, and they will work very hard to make sure they win against all obstacles.

The sign of Aries is ruled by the planet Mars, and the god of war symbolism is more than coincidence—the sign is as much a warrior as the planet guiding the journey. When a planet travels through Aries, it is driven toward greater outward expression of its natural influence.

Taurus

The second sign in the zodiac is Taurus, the bull. Taurus is known to be stubborn ("bull-headed"), stable, practical, and deliberate; you won't find very many flighty Taurus people. The sun moves into Taurus on approximately April 20 each year and stays until May 20. The cardinal Aries brought forth the season of spring, but once we move into the fullness of spring, the personification of the season is the fixed earth energy of Taurus. When the sun journeys through Taurus, it is an ideal time for earth-related magic. In my personal practice, I associate the season of spring with the element of Earth (summer with fire, autumn with water, and winter with air) and people have asked me why, as many modern Witches link winter with earth and spring with air. The reason I do it differently is because of this astrological placement. The time of Taurus is the time of active, fertile earth in the northern hemisphere whereas in winter, the earth is dormant. I'm not advocating for one method over another; actually using both makes the most sense. Harnessing the power of active earth for growth and healing during spring and drawing in passive earth energy for introspection, meditation, grounding, and renewal during winter time both have merit.

With all this talk of earth energy, it should be noted that Taurus is ruled by the planet Venus, which shows its stable and achievement-focused side through Taurus's love of creature comforts and fine living. When a planet travels through Taurus, it is guided toward expressing its energy in a steady manner; even unorthodox thinking or methods are still done in a sensible, deliberate fashion.

Gemini

This is the third sign of the zodiac, and it is the sign of communication. Gemini strives to know "why." It is ruled by Mercury and the planet of communication lends this sign tremendous mental agility. Gemini is "the twins" and as such is a dual sign that has the nature of neutrality, an integration of both yin and yang energies. A mutable air sign, Gemini begins the process of shifting away from spring and readying the environment for summer. When a planet travels through Gemini, its energy is channeled toward disseminating information, gathering truth, and expressing it to the world.

Cancer

The fourth astrological sign, Cancer, is ruled by the moon and considered the mother of the zodiac. Even the men born in this sign usually have a strong capacity for nurturing and "mothering" friends and relatives. The cardinal water sign, Cancer is well skilled in initiating emotional change. The symbol for this sign is the crab, alluding to a tendency toward moodiness but also incredible strength. This is a powerful sign that brings forth the summer season; the Sun enters Cancer on the Summer Solstice, an incredibly magical time.

Cancers are very home and family oriented, and they have a talent for bringing out the best in those for whom they have affection; they are very protective people. When planets travel through Cancer, energies are channeled toward empathy, connection, counseling, lunar energy, femininity, and emotional expression.

♌ Leo

This sign is ruled by the sun. Leo is fixed fire, personifying the energy of the summer in full swing. Fire signs in general are energetic people, and the Leo is no exception. Though full of energy, there is a tendency to seek out comfort and relaxation, perhaps due to the fact that the sign of Leo occurs during the hottest part of the year—vacation time! Leos love luxury, even more than Taurus and seeks to live like royalty. Ruled by the sun, they usually radiate confidence and bravado though an inclination toward arrogance must be avoided.

Symbolized by the lion, Leo is the sign of pride and loyalty. Most Leos will remain loyal to a friend or loved one through the most difficult of circumstances. There are really only two ways to lose the loyalty of a Leo: belittle them or betray their trust. Leos are usually not about to give a second chance for such an offense. When planets travel through Leo, their energies are channeled to creativity, performance, power, dramatic expression, leadership, independence, and accumulation.

♍ Virgo

This is the sign of greatest efficiency. Like Gemini, Virgo is ruled by Mercury. Where the Gemini Mercury is about expressive communication for the sheer joy of it, the Virgo Mercury is more about productive communication, sharing information to determine what is useful and what is unnecessary or extraneous. Virgo is mutable earth; born during harvest, the Virgo excels in productive work. Aside from industry and efficiency, Virgo also rules over health and nutrition, pets, and self-discipline.

Virgo is an intellectual and independent sign that enjoys problem-solving and being of help to others. Their focus is usually on progress, and they have little time or patience for disruptions or frivolousness. The symbol for Virgo is the virgin holding a stalk of harvest grain. The virgin symbolizes independence (the "virginity" here means belonging only to the self), purity of mind, and transformation. When planets travel through this sign, their energy is channeled toward critical thinking, analysis, learning, teaching, service, efficiency, work, and detail.

♎ Libra

Much like Taurus, which is also ruled by Venus, Libra loves beauty and the finer things in life. However, the Venus energy of Libra is more relationship-oriented than its Taurus expression. Libra is the sign of partnership, relationship, and union—Libras love to be in a couple. This is also the sign of balance, justice, equality, and diplomacy. The symbol of Libra is the scales, and people born in this sign strive to achieve equilibrium. Libra is known to have trouble making decisions, but they excel in conflict resolution and negotiation.

Libra is a social and usually good-natured sign that is intellectual (due to its air sign nature) despite being ruled by Venus, the planet of love and feeling. When planets transit through the sign of Libra, their energy is channeled toward cooperation, balance, love, harmony, networking, etiquette, sharing, and beauty.

♏ Scorpio

Intensity is the watchword for Scorpio. This is the most intense sign of the zodiac. Ruled by Pluto, Scorpio is the embodiment of transformation. In an ironic paradox (as Scorpio is the fixed water sign), Scorpios tend to dislike change even though their nature encourages it. Of the water signs, this one is the personification of the phrase "still waters run deep." Scorpio can seem very shy and distant, but they have a depth of emotion few can match. Their ruler, Pluto is the slowest planet and as such always has the upper hand in planetary aspects. Scorpio's secondary ruler is Mars, the planet of conflict and force. With this combination of planets, the energy of Scorpio is that of unstoppable force (also see Capricorn).

Unlike the other signs, Scorpio actually has three symbols; the scorpion, the snake, and the phoenix. The scorpion symbolizes Scorpio's protective and defensive nature; the deadly sting used only during extreme danger since it, like the sting of a bee, costs the user its life. This sign has great power but must remember to use it carefully lest they self-destruct. The snake symbolizes the sign's stealth, wisdom, and sexuality, as Scorpio rules sex. The phoenix symbolizes the intense power of transformation this sign wields.

Scorpio is a powerful sign with a depth that can sometimes be too much for even them to handle. Their intensity is tempered by their strength of emotion due to their water element. When planets are moving through this sign, their energies are channeled toward transformation, investigation, intensity, sexuality, strength, force, and desire.

Sagittarius

This sign is the sign of aspiration and philosophy. Sagittarians always seek to expand their horizons and reach new levels of understanding and enlightenment. Free spirited and inquisitive, a Sagittarius is almost always a great lover of travel, forever craving new experiences and adventures. Given their mutable fire nature, this sign can be restless and impatient but is hardly ever difficult or uncompromising. Ruled by Jupiter, they seek freedom, expansion, growth, and knowledge. Higher education, religions, philosophy, travel, optimism, and teaching are all natural to this sign.

The symbol of Sagittarius is the centaur, half-man, half-horse, a symbol said to represent the desire to rise above animal instinct and reach new heights. When planets travel through this sign, their energies are channeled toward growth, expansion, luck, learning, teaching, philosophy, religion, optimism, reaching goals, and personal improvement.

Capricorn

This is the cardinal earth sign; the energy that initiates winter. Capricorn is ruled by Saturn, the timekeeper and planet of restriction and binding. Theirs is the energy of "immovable object" in contrast to the energy of Scorpio. I have observed that these two signs appear to comprise a great cosmic interplay; the light and dark serpents of the Caduceus or the white and black pillars of the High Priestess Tarot card. Even though these signs are unrelated, they have a startling magnetic quality to one another both in attraction and repulsion; the OD and OB energies found in Eliphas Levi's book *Transcendental Magic* that represent free will and fate.

Capricorn is the sign of fate and time. Though Scorpio yearns to transcend and thus understand and conquer every state of being, it is Capricorn who holds the key. This sign rules age, time, achievement, career, destiny, ambition, accomplishment, organization, restriction, and discipline. Capricorn is the natural ruler of the tenth house, which is considered to be at the top of the astrological chart (the mid-heaven placement) and so is of prime importance in determining a person's level of success and reputation. For a person born with an Aries sun sign or rising sign, Capricorn is their mid-heaven sign. For the rest of us, whichever sign occupies our mid-heaven placement, assumes the role of the tenth house.

Though they may at times have a tendency to be pessimistic or stern, Capricorn people never lose their drive to achieve. This sign is symbolized by the goat and/or the mythical sea-goat, an animal of strong endurance that can survive famine and treacherous climbs up sheer cliff faces to reach its goal at the top of the mountain, perfectly underscoring Capricorn's ambitious nature. When planets travel through this sign, their energy is channeled toward greater accomplishment and drive, practicality, discipline, binding and banishing, time management, longevity, and success against all odds.

♒ Aquarius

Where Capricorn represents fate, Aquarius brings change. It is curious to note that both Aquarius and Scorpio are fixed signs, yet theirs is the energy of change. Aquarius is the fixed air sign, and it is the dominant force of winter. This sign is ruled by Uranus and is all about innovation and discovery. The Aquarius person is usually very community oriented, seeking to merge the needs of the individual with the needs of the group for the benefit of all.

Aquarius is the sign of humanitarianism, invention, discovery, ingenuity, imagination, and originality. The symbol of Aquarius is the water-bearer; a kneeling human figure pouring water from two jugs, said to represent knowledge flowing down to humanity. The symbol underscores Aquarian drive, to contribute something of lasting value to the greater community. When planets travel through Aquarius, their energies are channeled toward unique expression, flashes of genius, electricity, invention, unconventional thinking, new ideas, and the unexpected.

Pisces

The last sign of the zodiac is the mutable water sign of Pisces. This sign is ruled by Neptune and is attuned to dreams, fantasy, psychic experience, dissolution, compassion, altruism, the subconscious, and transcendent spirituality. Pisces is considered the end of the astrological cycle; the last stage of the journey before the rebirth of Aries and a new cycle. Being the culmination of the journey, this sign is frequently very psychic and has a deep "inner knowing" and maturity. Being both mutable and water, Pisces has an incredible emotional sensitivity and nearly endless capacity for nurturing.

The symbol for Pisces is twin fishes connected by a cord said to symbolize the two sides of the mind linked together, resulting in psychic power. Their sensitivity leads Pisces to altruistic pursuits but can also lead to flights of fancy or in difficult cases, the seeking of escape from reality through substance abuse. When planets travel through Pisces, their energies are channeled toward psychic expression, dissolution, merging, intuition, faith, spirituality, creativity, dreams, illusions, and love.

Planetary Aspects

As the planets orbit the sun, from our vantage point, they form what are known as *aspects*, that is, when the planets come within a certain mathematical degree of one another from our vantage point on earth. Each zodiac sign is divided into thirty degrees and the number of degrees that planets are apart from each other determines their aspect. The different points correspond with different energy flows; some are considered positive and others negative. The primary aspects are as follows: conjunction, sextile, square, trine, and opposition.

Conjunction

When one or more planets are conjunct to another planet, they are orbiting between zero and ten degrees of each other. They are almost always in the same sign and tend to amplify that sign's energy. This aspect is usually considered beneficial, though with "difficult" planets like Saturn, Mars, and/or Pluto, a conjunction can bring added stress to a sign. Regardless, it is the most powerful of aspects. When you want to channel the peak energy of the planets in question, it is best to catch them in conjunction.

Sextile

A sextile occurs when planets are 60 degrees apart from each other. This is an aspect of smooth communication between the planets. Though not the most powerful, this aspect is excellent for creating new opportunity using the energy of the planets involved.

Square

When planets are 90 degrees apart, they are said to be squared to each other. This is a difficult aspect of blocked communication. There is disharmony in the energy expressed, so one should avoid calling upon the energies of the planets in this aspect for any positive purpose. Now, a square doesn't mean "don't do any magic" during this type of aspect; I only mean to say that it isn't the time of greatest planetary energy output. The easiest example is the sun and moon: square to each other twice each month during the first quarter and third quarter moons, they are certainly not the peak times of solar and lunar power though these times can be used for magic.

Trine

When planets are 120 degrees apart, they are trine to each other. This is a most positive aspect. A trine expresses harmony and ease. Each planet in the aspect reinforces the powers of the other, ideal for creative endeavors, clear communication, and any positive magic.

Opposition

The hardest aspect occurs when the planets involved are 180 degrees apart from each other, essentially opposite one another in the wheel of the zodiac. This aspect is the polar opposite of the conjunction and is contradictory and exaggerating in nature whereas a conjunction provides unification and clarity. Opposition is usually considered a negative aspect, but this is not always so—the moon is full when in opposition to the sun. Basically an opposition means there is a greater force of energy from one planet to another, and the outer planet always "wins" the battle.

As an example, let's say that Pluto in Capricorn is in opposition to Mercury in Cancer. Mercury, ruler of communication, would be at a great disadvantage to Pluto, ruler of transformation and the farthest, slowest planet. Communication, especially for Cancers, would be difficult; outbursts and misunderstandings would be more likely to happen during an aspect's transition. If, however, you are trying to magically influence someone born under the sign of Cancer to leave you alone or stop gossiping, using the energy of Pluto to bear down on them would be powerful and effective. Oppositions can be powerful and useful as long as you channel the energy in the proper direction. It is no use to try and channel the energy of the lower planet to that of the higher...it is like pushing a boulder up a hill.

The Stars: Polaris, Aldebaran, Regulus, Antares and Fomalhaut

Aside from the stars as they relate to the zodiac, there are many other specific stars that have been highly regarded by Witches and others for thousands of years. Five of these stars are considered critical points in the cosmos, and their energy is said to affect our lives in various ways. The first star discussed is considered the single point of stillness in an ever-turning sky: Polaris, the North Star.

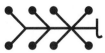 ### *Polaris*

This star is known as Polaris and the North Star. It is also called the Pole Star, Lodestar, Stella Maris, Star of the Mountain, and the Guiding Star. This star stands in near perfect alignment with the axis of Earth's rotation and so appears motionless with all the other stars in the sky rotating around it. The fixed nature of this star from our vantage point has been true from only about the year 500

CE. Due to the shifting of the earth's rotation (axial precession), it appears to slowly move through a gravitational shift similar to the wobbling of a spinning top with our celestial pole moving approximately every 26,000 years. Regardless, Polaris is always in the north near the pole and has historically been regarded as a great fixed point, the marker of alignment to the cardinal directions, since the rest of the cosmos appears to revolve around it. The North Star can be used magically to help us reconnect to the earth, the sacred land, and also to ancestral power, higher beings, and personal destiny.

Though this star marks the north, it is also quintessentially up and above and even a center point from which to draw strength. It has been seen mythically as the shining star above the top of the axis mundi, the World Tree.[2] If we were standing at the North Pole, the star would be above us; from our perspective it could be seen as the metaphorical keystone in the arch of the cosmos. Given its fixed nature, wherever we are in the northern hemisphere we can look to Polaris to reorient ourselves not only to north but (by extension) also to east, south, and west; finding north clues us in to all points. We can connect with the North Star in meditative work designed to connect with higher beings as the North Star has been viewed as a sacred point due to the fact the entire sky appears to revolve around it. In a magic circle, a simple means of using this star's power is to call it in as the center point. After the circle is cast

2 Cassandra Eason, *A Complete Guide to Night Magic* (New York: Citadel Press, 2002), 67.

but before the quarters are called, a candle can be lit or the Polaris symbol can be placed in the center of the circle with a visualization of either a column of energy pouring down from the star through the top of the circle or the world tree growing up from the ground through the circle with its branches reaching out to touch the star. This is a useful means of paving the way for higher energies to be drawn to your working. It builds an astral bridge from the heavens to the earth. Once the visualization is complete, the quarters can be called, any chosen deities can be invoked, and the ritual can proceed. Before opening the circle after the rite, dissolve the visualization. If a candle was used, snuff it out to break the connection to the star.

The North Star has a stature above most correspondences. It is associated with several deities such as the Welsh Arianrhod, the Irish Eithniu, and the Norse/Germanic Aesir deities. Polaris is connected to (yet above and beyond) all seasons and elements. Its colors are white, violet, and orchid. Judeo-Christian associations vary, though some connect the Archangel Raphael to Polaris; it is also sometimes associated with the Virgin Mary and the star on top of a Christmas tree.

The Guardians of the Watchtowers

"The who of the what?" That was my question, at least. When I first heard this term, I was already familiar with the concept of elementals, spiritual guardians, astral familiars, and all kinds of beings—and it was this way in which these guardians were depicted. My first encounter was a while ago, back when the Internet barely existed and the limited books to which I had access were not very helpful in this regard. In my own tradition, the Watchtowers are not used and the only available information about them was something to the effect of "those are Greek practices, not Celtic, so we don't use them." Far from satisfying my curiosity, I tried digging deeper.

Eventually, I learned the guardians were stars that had been revered for millennia, even in ancient Mesopotamia. These particular stars were held in high regard because they were the brightest stars in the constellation that personified whatever season each star could be visible. Each star is viewed as the guardian of a specific season, direction, and elemental force. The watchtower reference is twofold: "watchtower" denotes a protective force, and according to some authors (particularly Raven Grimassi) the ancient stellar cults who revered these stars built towers to honor them when giving offerings and prayers.[3] When properly channeled, the light and power of these stars channeled can serve as effective boundaries of security that keep out any harmful entities or energies that could disrupt your rites, metaphorically and magically speaking. The symbols listed for each of these watchers are star runes, and their use is attributed to hereditary Italian Witches.[4] These stars and their alignments are as follows:

---

3 Raven Grimassi, *Hereditary Witchcraft* (St. Paul, MN: Llewellyn Worldwide, 1999), 226–227.

4 Ibid. 148–150.

Aldebaran

This is the brightest star in the constellation of Taurus, the fixed earth sign. When seasonal alignments were originally determined, this star marked the Vernal Equinox (the sun was conjunct with Taurus), and so Aldebaran was considered the Watcher of the East. My personal assertion that springtime is best for working with the active power of the fertile Earth element as opposed to only working with Air is supported by the association here. So the Watcher of the East is also aligned with Earth since it is the brightest star of an earth sign.

To most who work with this system, the Watcher of the East is associated with the element of air, the colors white and yellow, the elemental sylphs, and to those with Judeo-Christian leanings, the Archangel Raphael (much more than with the North Star).

Regulus

This is the brightest star in the constellation of Leo, the fixed fire sign. This star is the Watcher of the South. Its element is fire, and it marks the season of summer. The Watcher of the South is associated with the colors red and orange, the salamander elementals, and the Archangel Michael.

Antares

This is the brightest star in Scorpio, the fixed water sign. Antares is the Watcher of the West and marks the season of Autumn. This Watcher is associated with the element of water, the colors blue, gray and black, undine elementals, and the Archangel Gabriel.

Fomalhaut

This is the brightest start in the constellation of Piscis Austrini, the "southern fishes" though this constellation is within the astrological sign of Aquarius, the fixed air sign. Ptolemy ascribed this star as belonging to both Piscis Austrini as the eye of the fish, but it is also between the feet of Aquarius. Either way, it is the Watcher of the North. Personally, I would associate it with Air since it is in the sign of Aquarius, but to most it is considered to be aligned with the Earth element. This Watcher is given the colors brown, green, and black, as well as gnome elementals and the Archangel Uriel. Sometimes, you may see Fomalhaut given the alternate spelling of "Foralhaut."

When it comes to the Guardians of the Watchtowers, the consensus seems to be that ancient stellar cults regarded these stars as gods, evolved and far removed from the world so that they guard the four quadrants of the universe from the stars in which they reside. The later Greeks demoted them to belonging to the gods of the four winds; Boreas of the north wind, Eurus of the east wind, Notus of the south wind, and Zephyrus of the west wind. From there, the Judeo-Christian religions related them to four Archangels, under which rulership other angels belonged.

Whatever system you choose to use, it is important to be cognizant of the basic properties of and alignments with the Watchers, elementals, cardinal directions, and any other force you want to call into your ritual space. It is wise to avoid calling in random unknown forces into your rites and spells if you can help it. Knowing what you are calling and why doesn't help much unless we know how to do it.

Call Upon Planetary and Stellar Energies

Though evoking and channeling the energies of planets and stars sounds like a daunting and impossible task, it is actually relatively simple due to the properties of light and energy. The fact of the matter is that the energies we draw upon from the planets or stars in ritual are already here on Earth. Even though our focus during the call is on the chosen celestial body in its far away location, we are in reality absorbing the energy that has already reached our planet from the distant planet or star. Since light and its corresponding rays travel in infinite directions and we can see the planets or stars from our vantage point on Earth (even if we have to use a telescope), the light is reaching us continually; otherwise the celestial body would appear to vanish. Since their energies are reaching us on Earth in a continual stream much like sunlight, we can call upon their power at a local level whenever we choose regardless of whether or not we are looking at the star while we are doing it.

There are many different ways to draw in energy and power; celestial energies can be called using a variety of methods, most of which employ the concept of correspondence (see chapter 5 for more on this principle). In this context, correspondence is a close similarity, connection, or equivalence that uses traditional associations between colors, directions, plants, crystals, minerals, metals, and symbols of each planet and star or constellation. No matter what sort of spell is being cast, planetary energies via correspondences can be included to boost the spell's power.

There are intense, complicated, highly involved ceremonial magic rituals designed to capture the essence of planetary energies into talismans involving the creation of mathematical sigils (special symbols drawn through the correspondence of numbers, letters, and the planet), but those techniques are too extensive to cover in this chapter. Fortunately, a much simpler method of harnessing celestial energies through the use of symbols makes use of the power of candle magic. Selecting a candle in a color appropriate to the planet or star's nature while visualizing a magical goal, carve the symbol of the planet or star onto one side of the candle. On the other side, carve your goal in words or a personal symbol that represents the goal to you. Next, the candle can be anointed with an appropriate planetary or stellar oil (see chapter 14) rubbing from both ends to the middle. Now, speak to the celestial body as if it were a person standing before you and ask that your candle be energized with its energy. An example to Jupiter could be: "Mighty Jupiter, on this night and in this hour, please fill this candle with your power. Growth, expansion, wealth, success; with good fortune, I am blessed." After calling on the planet, the candle can be lit and the energy released.

This simple spell can be enhanced with planetary or stellar incense (see chapter 14), and related crystals and herbs can be placed in circles around the candle to magically feed it with power. These symbols can also be placed in appropriately colored charm bags that can themselves be charged with the planet's magical force. The bag can be carried to radiate the spell's power.

FIVE

Know Your Craft

When we first dedicate ourselves to the study of Witch-craft, whether it be as solitary practitioners or under the guidance of a teacher, we learn magical rules and laws such as the Threefold Law or the Law of Return, which are related and sometimes conflated principles. Later in the training, we learn things like the importance of polarity and correspondence, the power of magical thought and vibration. However, not every student is given the fullness of the magical laws. Most magic laws can be traced to Hermetic laws in one way or another; those seven principles that purport to explain how the universe operates and how a person can work within the laws to change their environment through practical application.

These laws are said to be the teachings of Hermes Tris-megistus ("thrice-great"), who himself is said to be the merged amalgam of the Greek Hermes, the Roman Mercury, and the

Egyptian Thoth, all of whom relate to wisdom, travel, writing, and mediating between opposites. As with many things spiritual, there is debate as to when exactly Hermetic writings originated: the date varies anywhere between 500 BCE to 200 CE, and no one is certain to whom credit can be given as the human scribe(s) of these teachings. Nevertheless, they have stood the test of time and are an integral facet of many forms of "Western Esoteric Tradition." Mystical orders such as the Rosicrucians and (of course) the Hermetic Order of the Golden Dawn use them, and in one form or another, the Hermetic teachings have influenced modern Paganism.

One of the classic works intended to clarify and explain Hermetic philosophy is a book entitled *The Kybalion: A Study of the Hermetic Philosophy of Ancient Egypt and Greece,* first published in 1908 by the Yogi Publication Society. This book has been republished many times over the years and is easily obtainable today. Its authorship remains shrouded in mystery as it is credited to "Three Initiates" who chose to remain anonymous. Regardless of who wrote the book—and there is plenty of speculation on that topic—the *Kybalion* remains a valuable resource of Hermetic philosophy that can be used as a foundation for building a personal understanding of (and working relationship with) our own higher potential as well as the greater forces of nature and divinity.

The Hermetic Laws

These laws do not belong to a particular religion so much as they are general metaphysical thought. Hermetic philosophy claims itself to be an underlying unifying truth within all forms of religion and spirituality; it can be folded into many spiritual practices without conflict. In the *Kybalion,* the authors do not deny the existence of many gods or ascended masters, nor do they object to the veneration of such beings. They posit that there is an intriguing nature in most higher powers in the universe. This theory is stated in the first Hermetic principle, relating to the method of creation of the universe itself.

The Law of Mentalism

The Law of Mentalism states that since the first being, the creator deity—whom they term "the All"—is in fact all that is and the totality of existence. The only way the universe could have been created was through the power of the mind (the understanding is that there weren't any raw materials to use or any room beyond the All, as that would defy the definition). The Law of Mentalism states that the entire universe is mental in existence, that the All created it as a mental projection; a thought-form manifested in its mind. The Divine Mind has created everything in existence and so all the universe is interconnected down to the tiniest particle of matter. Everything is composed of the Divine's mental energy.

Because all things are mental in nature, our own minds are linked with the divine. We have access to spiritual knowledge and psychic phenomena in equal proportion to all other beings. The only reason we are not constantly flooded with all knowledge is that our senses filter out extraneous information; our eyes can only see so much of the spectrum, our ears can only hear a certain range of frequencies, and so on. Our individual minds could not possibly handle continual awareness of literally everything, which is why the mind has different facets: the conscious, subconscious, and unconscious, respectively. The techniques seers, Witches, shamans, and other mystics employ (such as meditation, trance, divination, and ritual) seek to temporarily open the filters of our senses to allow a greater influx of information into our consciousness.

Understanding this Law of Mentalism is seen as a master key to unlocking true comprehension and command of the other Hermetic principles. Even though, the universe may be mental in character, it still operates according to the other laws of nature and these are expressed through the other six Hermetic principles. The Law of Mentalism states how the universe exists and what it is made of, whereas the other laws explain how it operates.

The Law of Correspondence

This law is an integral part of nearly every magical practice. Examples of practical applications of the Law of Correspondence include sympathetic magic such as the use of a poppet, any spell involving herbal ingredients, the use of elemental tools like the chalice and athame; really any action that makes use of symbolism or alignment with higher forces (or lower for that matter) because we are employing the maxim: "as above, so below." This law is important to the understanding of the natures and interplay of mental, physical, and spiritual phenomena. It has been observed that the manner in which the greater macrocosm operates has a direct parallel in our lives on Earth. This is the basis for and secret of astrology; the planetary interactions do not "make" something happen; they offer clues about the predominant trends in the larger solar system and the smaller microcosm of our own lives. As above, so below; as the universe, so also the soul. It is true in much more than a symbolic sense.

As research progresses particularly in the field of quantum physics, the body of evidence that the Hermetic Laws are in fact genuine from not only a magical but also a scientific sense is increasing, although scientists are a bit unwilling to admit it. It has been determined that human beings share an incredible amount of similarities with much of the rest of the planet. It is said that more than 90 percent of our DNA is the same as that of a fly; according to *National Geographic* we as a species even share 25 percent of the same genes as rice.[5] While in much of human history it has been customary to focus on obvious differences between plants, animals, and humans—thus making it much easier to exploit those considered "lower" in the hierarchy—it is now scientifically

---

5 Carl Zimmer, *National Geographic*, July 2013 "Genes are Us. And Them"

understood that humans are not especially separate and superior to nature. We are all in fact made of the same genetic stuff, part of the greater whole.

I would be remiss if I didn't qualify my statement by noting that I'm not saying that having a bowl of rice is tantamount to cannibalism or that there aren't important differences in nature and intelligence between most human beings and the average housefly. Much of the DNA we share with the vast majority of the natural world is basic, not the more sophisticated genes that give us reasoning and language skills well beyond a coral reef or a banana tree. However, it is theorized that all of us—yeast, rice, cat, ape, dolphin, or human— share an original common ancestor that lived more than 1.6 billion years ago, and every lineage descended from that progenitor has retained parts of its original genome. The idea that humans share genetic similarities to other creatures on Earth would have been considered an absurd heretical statement or vicious lie only a short decade ago, but the fact remains that we all share a genetic bond.

The power of correspondence lies in the similarities shared between all things. For example, the reason quartz crystals and moonstone are used to channel lunar energy is their coloring and that they are believed to resemble the moon. And the reason that quartz and moonstone actually do channel lunar power is not only because of their color and appearance but also that both are rich in silica, as is the moon's surface; as above, so below. What was originally discovered intuitively is more often than not found to have material basis. Iron is a metal spiritually attributed to Mars. This was because iron rusts and turns red and Mars is the red planet. Hundreds of years ago it was not understood why iron turned red nor was it known that Mars is red is due to its iron oxide-rich soil, so the Martian soil is basically rust-red. Again we see intuitive understanding having material basis.

The Law of Correspondence is all about relation and potential. Returning to the subject of DNA, we can think of stem cells as magical, for these cells carry the information to become any type of cell; they contain the fullness of genetic potential. The cell could be anything but it becomes what it needs to become based on the correspondence of the surrounding tissue in a perfect display of magical transformation. When they reach an injured part of the body and go about repairing the injury by becoming new tissue of the type needed, they are manifesting relation and potential. Everything is contained within everything else.

The reason tables of correspondence have been created over the years is to make readily available lists of items with related properties so we can more easily create pathways for magic. We set our intention in the microcosm and release the vision into the greater macrocosm through the charging of ingredients which have natural correspondences to our magical goal or the greater forces we are petitioning for assistance.

The Law of Vibration
Everything in the universe is in motion; nothing is static. All things move according to their own rate of vibration. These

rates of vibration are unique expressions of motion based on the type and quality of the energy or matter in question. Scientifically, it is believed that if an object were to reach the speed of light it would cease to be matter and instead become pure light energy itself; that its rate of vibration would be so high that it would no longer maintain its former structural integrity. Magically speaking, this is the explanation for the differing levels of existence from pure spirit—considered the highest vibration—all the way down to gross physical matter. As physical beings, we have bodies composed of matter but we also have subtle bodies such as the etheric and astral bodies corresponding to different planes and rates of vibration. Our brain waves oscillate at differing vibrations depending on our level of awareness, whether we are awake or asleep, and our stress level. The various states of matter are not really solid but actually energy moving at different rates of vibration, which is true all the way down to the subatomic level. If we employ the Law of Correspondence, we can deduce that the Law of Vibration is also true all the way up to the furthest reaches of the universe and beyond.

The Law of Polarity

This teaching is perhaps the most important of the Hermetic laws relating to magical practice. This law states that everything is dual in nature and has poles. This is most easily expressed in magnetism and heat, but is said to be true of all things and states of being. It is considered that all things have their opposites and that these opposites are really the extreme poles of the same thing differing only in degree. Consider: where does "hot" end and "cold" begin? Where does left become right, up become down, love become hate or good become evil? It is a very necessary teaching that all opposites can be reconciled. Some of the greatest truths not only of Witchcraft but also in the greater context of life can be found through the resolution of paradoxes. The veil of perception and semantics must be pierced so that we can truly see the underlying concepts and realities to be able to change anything about it.

Polarity can be shifted. This is the actual process of magic, the transmutation of a thing or situation from one end of its polarity to the other. In other instances, the target of the magic can be transmuted anywhere along the line of polarity between the extremes including the center point, which has a neutral quality. When something is neutralized, it is at the calm gray between black and white, so to speak. As with all the other laws, the Law of Polarity works in kinship with the Law of Vibration. The high rate of particle vibration that is heat is the upper pole of temperature whereas a low rate of vibration is cold. To alter polarity in this case is to change the rate of vibration. It must be noted that polar transformation only works according to all the other natural laws; no one can turn a banana into a space heater, but it is possible to raise our vibration such that we can feel warm even if the weather is chilly. Likewise, we can turn a curse into a blessing, fear into courage, anything negative into a positive; all that's needed is to shift the vibration to its opposite pole.

The Law of Rhythm

As before, this law builds on the ones before it. The Law of Rhythm illustrates two things; the balance and harmony of existence and also how, if everything is a manifestation of vibration, more than one type of thing exists in the universe. Rhythm is the measured motion between extremes. It is pattern within vibration. Everything has inflow and outflow, rise and fall, flow and ebb. Not accounting for friction, the distance of a pendulum's swing in one direction equals the distance in the other; basic physics shows the balance within rhythm.

The Law of Rhythm also shows that even though all things are vibration, they resonate at differing rates, sort of how televisions have many channels because though the signals are all the same type of waves, they are different frequencies and act as independent channels. If they had the same rhythm, the signals would be an unreadable combination of broadcasting. The Law of Rhythm keeps things in check. Though we are all vibration, human beings do not vibrate at the same rate as water or metal or chickens. Each type of being or phenomena has what could be considered a frequency range within which it manifests in reality. For example, chickens are not humans because their energy does not vibrate within the same range as people; similarly, my friends and I are not all the same person because our individual frequencies differ from each other though we all fall within the human range.

The Law of Rhythm is the "why" behind the cycle of life Witches mark in ritual. Far from being a silly superstition, it is believed that in celebrating the sabbats, Witches are participating in the turning of the wheel of the year, the shifting of nature's cycle. This belief has a scientific equivalent in the "Observer Effect" a scientific principle stating that the act of observation will make changes on a phenomenon being observed. As an example, this is seen in particle physics when attempting to observe electrons. In order for an electron to become observable, a photon must interact with it and this alters the course of the electron by default. When we actively participate in rhythm, we can help to encourage its positive manifestations and can become less subject to its negative consequences.

The Law of Cause and Effect

If everything is mental in nature and vibrates according to rhythm, oscillating from one end of polarity to the other and is linked together through correspondence, then the truth of the Law of Cause and Effect becomes clear. For every action is an equal and opposite reaction according to both Newton's third law of motion and the Hermetic Laws. Everything is interconnected so that what affects one thing resonates through and creates a ripple effect, causing changes throughout the greater environment even if those changes are imperceptible to us at the time. The Law of Cause and Effect states that nothing occurs without cause and that there is no such thing as pure chance. There are varying planes of cause and effect, with the higher planes having dominion over the lower planes but all things are subject to the law.

It is from this law that the notion of there being no coin-
cidences originates, which is essentially true but must be quali-
fied with the understanding that though everything has a cause,
not every effect (or every cause) is intentional by its originator.
No one on this level of existence has continuous full knowledge
of every facet of cause and effect; nobody can foresee the full
range of effect for every little mundane action or choice which
means that we are all subject to a great deal of unintentional
occurrences which our perception deems as coincidence. The
Law of Cause and Effect reveals a key secret becoming magical;
by projecting our desire in an intentional manner on a higher
plane of causation, we are able to create a purposeful ripple
effect designed to manifest our desire on this plane as a natural
effect of our projection and magical working.

When Witches work ritual and achieve the altered state of
consciousness necessary to cast a spell (often called the alpha state,
ritual consciousness, or the meditative state), we have raised our
vibration up on the scale of polarity to a higher level of causation.
The spell is worked and the programmed energy is projected into
this higher level, the spell is concluded and the practicing Witch
returns to normal awareness. Here, too, is where ethical considerations of magic come into focus. As stated earlier, the higher
planes of cause and effect dominate the lower planes. A Witch
may instigate change on this plane of existence but is still subject to the ripple effect through the higher planes. Nothing can
escape natural laws. The Law of Cause and Effect is also known
as the Law of Return; what goes around comes around. If the

energy we send out did not return to us, manifestation would be impossible. We receive as balance for that gift the consequences of our actions.

Luckily, any magical consequences generated are of the same polarity as the original action; in other words, positive magic brings about positive consequences and negative magic unleashes negative consequences. This is not a moral edict or judgment call on any sort of magic someone should practice, it is just natural law. There are times when a negative spell such as a binding or banishing is quite necessary even though some would argue against any such action. The trick to using such magic is doing so only if it is justified. If someone or something is causing harm then to work a binding or banishment is ultimately a positive action that corrects for harm and as such, does not generate the same type of negative return at the spell caster. The bottom line for the Law of Cause and Effect is that it is both the pathway for our spells to manifest and also the means by which the consequences of our actions return to us. Whether those consequences are beneficial or unfortunate is dependent on our choices.

The Law of Gender

The final Hermetic Law states that gender is in all things and manifests on every plane. The Law of Gender is a manifestation of the Law of Polarity. Within and beyond all things lies a creative energy that is expressed through both receptive and projective forces whose dynamic interplay is the generative cause of creation. Simply put, what are called feminine and masculine are the opposite poles of the same polarity, and their interactions are what result in creation. Active and passive energies seek their opposites in order to reconcile themselves and the level of balance between these forces is responsible for the differing frequencies of vibration described in the earlier laws.

Each living being (and all of existence) manifests both feminine and masculine aspects to its nature. When there is an exact balance between masculine and feminine, asexuality or gender neutrality is the result. Many plants and animals are asexual in their reproduction; it is a natural manifestation of life. Androgynous or transgendered people, too, are natural manifestations of life. Speaking in magical terms, this results from having differing ratios of masculine and feminine forces within the individual than the more typical pattern of the predominant gendering that analogues with the person's sex at birth. In truth, we all have masculine and feminine components of our being. Each of us consciously identifies with our predominant gender expression; the opposite side is our latent inner nature. Seeking to consciously cultivate an awareness and link to our inner opposite lends us power—creation occurs through the interplay of these forces. This is the reason that some traditions of Witchcraft have placed much emphasis on "perfect working couples"—male and female pairs—but the male/female dynamic can actually be achieved within the self; the resulting magical ability is available to everyone. A person's opposite, their "anima" or "animus" as they have come to be called, can almost act as spirit guides or allies. It should be noted that contact and communication with our inner opposite is not about altering our sexuality or identity, but rather about expanding our consciousness and creative ability.

Sadly, the Law of Gender is a difficult subject to discuss without running the risk of sounding sexist in one way or another, homophobic, or transphobic. In truth, the Law of Gender rejects notions of hierarchy, favoring instead upholding the importance of diversity and the belief that gender is a scale or spectrum rather than a rigid "either/or" dynamic. It should not be ridiculed but understood. This law also serves as proof that each and every manifestation of gender and sexuality is a point on the scale of the polarity of gender. Without this polarity, creation would be impossible. The Hermetic Laws are spiritual guideposts for understanding the nature and pattern of the universe and also our own inner nature. When we use this knowledge, we can shape our lives *through* the universal laws instead of being shaped *by* them with little say in the matter.

Never Do Anything in Ritual If You Don't Know Why

That sounds bossy, doesn't it? I don't mean to negate the power of spontaneous ritual or say that a person has to know every last detail behind the cultural, historical, or mythical use of every ritual tool and ingredient in a spell before even trying a magical working. I think everyone would agree that it is a very good idea to have a basic working knowledge of the tools and words used in a spell as well as any required ingredients. As far as ingredients are concerned, familiarizing usually means making sure they all correspond to your magical goal. When it comes to the words used in ritual, it's best to only use the language you normally speak unless you know exactly what any words mean in any given spell written in another language. The reason is twofold: if the words aren't fully understood, it is difficult to ensure that the proper intent is being projected, and it's hard to know if you're pronouncing them properly.

Because a spell needs to be a projection of clear intent, it is so much more effective to have a streamlined ritual with only the basic necessities and familiar words than it is to have an overly complex, lengthy rite filled with archaic, confusing language and extraneous tools and ingredients. Having too much going on at once tends to muddle things and diffuse the intent.

The Altar as a Microcosm

When we use an altar, we are creating a focal point for a spell. Everything on the altar should be in alignment with our goal. The Hermetic Law of Correspondence states that what occurs in the microcosm has an effect on the macrocosm, so a properly constructed altar then becomes a microcosm of our own design, projecting exactly and only what we desire. Our magical altars should be tailored solely to our magical goals to avoid sending mixed messages. Admittedly, I like a beautiful, busy altar for religious ritual and daily devotionals, but for magic it is best to only have the items relating to the spell placed on the altar. That way, the energy of the entire altar is attuned to our message.

The same alignment requirement is also true of working tools. I love to use the tools, but if I'm not using one in the spell, I leave it off the altar. Not every spell uses every tool, and keeping them all on the altar as place holders distracts from the clarity of our intent. If we have a defined purpose to our altar, we create a powerful model, a template in the physical world for the astral plane to emulate and return to us in the form of our goal. It embodies perfectly the properties of "as above, so below" and cause and effect; we create a microcosm to influence the greater macrocosm which then in turn influences the microcosm. When we create an altar, we are creating a microcosm of how we want things to be *within* the structure of how things already are; we work within the established flow and pattern of the universe to manifest our will.

The Structure of Ritual

Whether it's a full scale ritual of celebration, a complex group working or a simple intuitive spell, a ritual usually includes certain steps to ensure success. Many, if not most Witches and spell casters use an energetic circle within which they work their rituals. When this circle is used, it can be cast intuitively or traditionally. An intuitive casting is usually more energetic and mental rather than methodical and ritualistic.

An example would be to sit in the middle of the ritual area, move into a meditative state, and once relaxed and ready, visualize an enveloping orb of energy around yourself and the working site in a circle of power. Once the circle is firmly visualized, then guardians or elementals can be called upon if desired and the rite or spell can proceed. A more traditional circle casting consists of several steps in specific order (there are variations) designed to ready the area for ritual. These steps include the following tasks.

Purification of Self

Not that we're "unclean" or "sinful"; purification in this sense means to remove all traces of energies that are not in harmony with our ritual goals in addition to any extraneous thoughts that may steal focus from our work. Self-purification generally takes the form of ritual bathing with the intent that the blessed and salted water draws out conflicting energies, leaving you refreshed and ready for magic. Besides a ritual bath, self-purification can take the form of pre-ritual grounding (see later this section), washing the hands in fast-running cold water (ideally scrubbing with salt at the same time), anointing with a purification oil, or encircling the body with a purification incense such as a blend of frankincense and myrrh. Whatever method is chosen, use it with intent and mental focus.

Cleansing the Area (Reiving)

Before a spell or ritual, it is a wise practice to physically and spiritually cleanse the area where the ritual will take place. Clutter can be a big distraction. If working indoors, it is a good idea to move furniture, rugs, plants, and anything else that may be in the way so that there is a suitable work environment. If you work outdoors, make sure there aren't any "presents" from animals on the ground, that there are no sharp objects, pointy sticks, holes, or other tripping hazards on the ground. If a fire is to be lit, ensure a proper and safe fire pit is dug. Next, the floor or ground should be vacuumed, swept, or raked as applicable to clear it of any debris. If indoors, remembering to turn off the phone and television would be appropriate at this time.

Once the cleaning is finished, the spiritual portion of the reiving can begin. A note about the word "reiving": while it is a word some Witches use to describe the process of cleansing the area of disruptive energies before a rite, its history is rather harsh. *Reive* is another word for "reave"; an archaic English word meaning to rob, despoil, deprive, seize, plunder, carry, or tear away. Though this sounds like an unusual word to use for cleansing, there is a certain amount of logic to it. The methods of reiving are considered disruptive, tearing away and rending asunder the negativity in an area; breaking it down so that it can be repolarized toward the positive or neutral end of the spectrum. An archaic word denoting destruction in a violent manner has been repurposed to indicate destruction in a cleansing and purifying manner.

Whatever the process is called, the spiritual portion of reiving can consist of one or more of the following: sweeping with the ritual broom perhaps with a visualization that the bristles are sending out energy to burn or blast apart any negativity, the sprinkling of saltwater to neutralize any negativity (only pure

water should be used outdoors), the ringing of a clear sounding bell, and/or encircling the area with a cleansing incense. If
using the ritual broom, the bristles needn't touch the ground in
order for cleansing to take place; the energy and intent are all
that matter. Once the reiving is complete, the next step is to set
up the altar.

Building the Altar and Ritual Area

The word *altar* need not be taken too literally. Depending on
the type of spell used, the altar can be a stove top, the kitchen
table, dresser top, TV tray, a portion of cleared ground, and so
on. If conducting a complicated, full-fledged ritual according
to many modern guidelines, an altar table should be placed
in the center of the working area, situated so it faces north.
There may also be smaller altars or at least markers, candles,
or offerings in each of the cardinal directions in honor of
the Watchtowers, elements, faery folk, or any other spiritual
allies or guardians chosen for the ritual. These altars should be
planned in advance, and all tools, items, and accessories should
be accounted for prior to the reiving. Once the altar is set up
according to the guidelines of the spell or ritual, it is best to
make sure that any extras such as matches, a small dish for used
matches, and anything else that could be needed are within the
area before actually casting the circle.

Casting the Circle

This is a step most practitioners know; my comments about
this step are thus limited. In general the circle is actually

cast by pointing a ritual blade, wand, or finger outward to the boundary of the circle and sending energy from the tool, creating a stream or curtain of power while walking the boundary in a clockwise direction to seal the area. In many instances, the circle is cast three times around to create the sacred space in all three realms of physical, mental, and spiritual energies.

Censing and Asperging the Circle

Though this step may seem redundant considering that incense and/or saltwater may have just been carried around the area in the reiving stage, this time salt, water, incense, and a lit altar candle are carried around the circle in order to prepare the environment for the calling of any guardians. A practitioner who works with watchers, guardians, or guides with elemental natures (as many Witches do), then fills the circle with the energies of physical manifestations of earth, air, fire, and water, which serves to bring resonance between the ritual area and the astral elemental essences. This process makes calling in elemental energies much easier and more effective.

Calling the Elements and/or Guardians

This step varies from tradition to tradition as there are so many customs specific to different regions. For example, an Irish Witch would have a different focus than, say, a Saxon Witch or a Strega when it comes to guardians, guides, and the elements. In our modern age, there are many who choose to explore the possibilities and change focus from one ritual to another; at one rite calling in elementals or faery folk while at the next calling on the Guardians of the Watchtowers, spirit animals, or even Judeo-Christian archangels.

No matter the chosen method, the important part is really cultivating a relationship with beings in a respectful manner and with as much understanding of their natures and the function we wish them to serve in the circle—watcher, guide, guardian, helper, elemental essence—are all different functions. Different beings have natural affinities for one function or another. The Watchtowers are distant and powerful, much more attuned to guardian status than magical helpers. Spirit animals are attuned to primal, outdoorsy magic as guardians or helpers. The elementals (gnomes, sylphs, undines, and salamanders) are beings of essence who are good for many different purposes and can be asked to guard or help lend their energies to the magic or even to carry the spell to its destination. Personally, I wouldn't advise calling on other nature spirits and faery folk since they can be unpredictable. If you already have a personal relationship with one or more faery folk, they can be called upon for assistance but until the relationship is cultivated they usually aren't that interested in our affairs.

Practically speaking, there are two different ways to invite any of these beings to your circle, inside or out. There are differing views on the merits of both options; some believe that inviting beings inside the circle increases the magical power available whereas others believe that keeping them outside the circle prevents any overabundance of energy within it. Particularly from the elementals, an excess of energy can bring problems with the physical elements themselves such as dangerously large or active candle flames. I have used both methods with equal success and haven't noticed any problems either way, but that's only my experience. If you wish to keep them on the outer perimeter of the circle, then any candles, offerings, or quarter altars should be placed just outside the circle's boundaries before it is cast. The beings can then be called upon at the appropriate time with you in the circle and them safely outside it.

Evocation and Invocation

If, in your spell or ritual, assistance from a deity is desired then this is the time to call upon them. Though there are varying definitions of these words, *evocation* here is defined as the calling of a spiritual power to manifest in your circle but outside yourself, and *invocation* is defined as the calling of a spiritual power to manifest within yourself. Evocation is how we usually call upon guardians or elementals. We can also evoke deities and ask that their energy grace our rite with power.

Invocation is more intimate and personal; it is an invitation to the Divine to connect and enter the practitioner's body. There are very complicated invocations using an "invoker" and an "invokee" such as in the calling down of the Goddess in the Drawing Down the Moon ritual, but for most purposes it is sufficient to speak to the chosen deity from the heart, asking that you be filled with their energy so your chosen goal can be realized.

The Spell or Ritual

After any invocations or evocations have taken place, we can finally conduct the spell or rite. Each spell has its own instructions but there are always the steps of visualizing the end result (thinking), while focusing strongly on the emotions you desire to have when the outcome is reached (feeling), and then projecting that emotion-infused energetic thoughtform outward to bring the goal into manifestation (willing). The unification of thought, emotion, and willpower creates the magical spark that moves each of those individual steps out of the realm of fantasy—dwelling in feelings, desire, or mere determination—and gives them the strength to create change.

Thanking the Deities, Elements, Guardians, and Guides

After the spell is cast, it is always proper respect to thank each god, guardian, or guide who has been called to the circle individually before the rite is concluded. Showing respect to the deities is common sense and good manners; showing respect to all of the beings called upon helps build a solid working relationship and also signals that the ritual is now winding down.

Concluding the Rite

After thanks are said, the ritual can be concluded. Usually candles are snuffed out in the reverse order they were lit (excluding the altar candles for illumination), and sometimes a bell is rung to signal the conclusion.

Grounding

After the rite has ended, it is wise to ground the excess energy within yourself and the circle. The meditative method or a visualization of energetic roots traveling down from your body into the earth that sends any excess energy through the roots can accomplish this. Afterward, pull the roots back into your body before opening the circle. An alternate method for grounding is to eat a small meal, but the food must be brought into the circle prior to the rite. Another method is to use a ritual blade, pentacle, wand, or chalice to absorb the excess energy by visualizing the energy being sucked into the tool and held there. These methods can be used individually or in combination, too.

Opening the Circle

After all the other steps have taken place, standing in the north and moving along the circle's inner perimeter, the circle can be cut with the ritual knife and the energy absorbed into the knife. Some practitioners only move clockwise both to cast the circle and to open it, whereas others cast it clockwise and then open it moving counterclockwise, reasoning that moving to the right creates positive energy and moving back to the left dissolves the energy. And some other people absolutely refuse to do anything counterclockwise, believing that it will attract negativity. It comes down to personal choice.

The directions are reversed entirely in the southern hemisphere, as the path of the sun is flipped horizontally. What those of us in the northern hemisphere would consider counterclockwise is the predominant positive motion in the southern hemisphere. Adapting to local energy patterns is always important.

Acting in Accord

The spell has been cast and the ritual ended. All that remains is to "act in accord," or conduct ourselves in such a way so as to find opportunities our magic has generated in order to bring about our goal. As has been said time and again, all the love spells in the world won't do any good if you never leave your house, answer the door or phone, or even use the Internet. We have to put ourselves in the right places for our spells to bear fruit. Magic certainly tips the odds in our favor but it can't make money appear in our hands; we have to seek the favorable circumstances in order to reach our goal. There are exceptions to this rule, but it is always good to act in such a way as to draw fortune and new opportunities to you; take chances without being too reckless and remain open to possibility.

Spellbinding and Sealing

Spellbinding is a manifestation of correspondence. To make a spell successful, a caster needs to have a link to the goal. When magic is directed toward a person, it is best to have an article of clothing, a lock of hair, fingernail clippings, a photograph, or (as a last resort) something they've written on or something they've touched. When using magic to influence a situation or manifest tangible items, it is important to have a symbol associated with your goal on the altar to help clarify the intent, focus the energy, and to create the psychic link. Using symbols is of course another method of correspondence and can be an important means of transferring energy, especially into a talisman.

Whether they be amulets of protection or talismans to create change or to bring needed items or opportunities, placing a symbol on or in the charm and charging it with energy serves not only to link your charm to your magical goal but also to bind the energy into the charm itself in order to seal the spell. Binding a charm's energy to seal it is a wise idea; if the energy is not bound strongly to the charm, it can bleed off and render the charm powerless. The sealing of an active spell (where the energy is sent out toward a goal) is usually in the form of physical movement or the drawing of a symbol in the air to affirm the energy has been sent and that the outflow is cut off. Popular forms of this include clapping the hands, drawing a pentagram with the athame or wand over the altar, striking the altar with the wand, and the ringing of a bell; whichever method is chosen, it is a good idea so as to break the connection between yourself and the magical power. Continuing an etheric connection to the spell after it is cast only serves to deplete your energy and cloud the spell's message and intent. Sealing a spell is a declaration—the magic is done!

Solitary Work versus Group Work

Working solitary has its advantages: when alone, we can do whatever we wish, are subject only to our desire, can get by with understanding the magical goal without needing to explain it to anyone else, and we can work at our own pace. We also have some disadvantages such as having only our skills and knowledge from which to draw inspiration, having less available energy to draw upon, having to contribute everything to the working by ourselves and so forth. In group work, the advantages include greater power available due to more participants, an expanded knowledge base, a sense of community, the powerful experience of the group mind, and the possibility of delegating tasks. Many hands make short work.

In solitary work, one is required to cast, call, bind, project, release, and ground. When working with others, certain precautions must be taken to preserve the magic's intent. Every aspect of the spell must be gone through like a rehearsal with others and the intent must be understood by all to prevent the message becoming confused. Each person must know what the goal is and how the visualizations and energy transmission will go so that everyone is all thinking and feeling the same thing at the same time throughout the spell process. Group spell work can be quite effective as long as the entire group understands the goals of the working, no one is particularly emotionally upset at the time, and no one is too ill to participate. Working magic when sick is possible but if the person is too ill, the release of energy can be too draining and is not a good idea. One last caution: only do magical workings with others if you have a good amicable relationship with them. Unresolved issues like resentments or anger undermine the working's effectiveness.

Working Outdoors

Conducting rituals outdoors is a valuable and wonderful experience. It can be powerful and spiritual and healing to work magic out on the open land. Centuries-old depictions of Witches show them outdoors for rituals usually dancing around a bonfire or a tree, and there is a reason for this: there are important magical aspects to working around these natural wonders.

Working Around a Bonfire

Fire in general is a powerful element, and a bonfire in particular can be a very strong channel for releasing magical energy. When working outdoors around a fire, it essentially becomes your altar. As such, it should ideally be composed only of woods that correspond to your magical goal or are suited for general magic; oak is a good choice. Herbs, symbols drawn on flat sticks or pieces of paper, burnable personal offerings such as images carved in wax, paper money, or items made of fabric, paper, or wood relating to your goal can all be placed in the fire to add energy to the spell.

When working in this way, it is traditional to dance around the fire to generate energy, building up power until you feel it is at its peak and then release it toward its goal. If this isn't desirable for some reason, the power can be raised other ways. After the ritual area is prepared but before the bonfire is lit, each of the woods, herbs and items can be charged with the magical intent and power summoned up from the earth into the spell caster using a meditation. Once the energy is at its peak, the bonfire can be lit. As it flares up, the programmed power within the spell caster can be released out toward the magical goal.

Working Around a Tree

Where a magical working around a bonfire is mainly focused on releasing energy, spells cast with the aid of a tree can work both ways, to send energy out and/or to draw it down. Trees are considered to be linked to all three realms: heavenly, physical, and the underworld. As such, energy can be sent or drawn through the tree to or from any of the realms. A great method of drawing down power can be used during the full moon. If you wait until the moon is high and its light is filtering through the tree branches, you can channel the lunar energy down through the tree and into your circle. This energy can then be absorbed by either dancing around the tree or by leaning against it and visualizing the power pouring into your body.

If it is desired to work a spell sending energy outward, it only needs to be programmed with intent and released back through the tree outward toward the goal. If the goal is spiritual in nature, it can be channeled up to the heavenly realm to contact higher beings. If the goal is related to elementals, nature spirits, the dead, or anything chthonic, the energy can be channeled through the roots to the underworld. If the goal is material in nature or relating to a specific person or event, the energy can be sent out through the tree into this physical realm.

Trees are living beings, and in this type of work they are essentially acting as spiritual allies. It is wise to ask the tree's permission in some way before conducting this work. You can connect with it using the exercise "Connect to a Tree" (on page 45), and when you feel the connection, ask for the tree's permission and assistance. Aside from being the polite thing to do, this action also helps to align the tree's energy flow to the rite's, starting things off in the correct manner.

PART TWO
Magical Practice

This section covers practical application of the natural laws and magical concepts in spellwork, making use of many different methods and practices that have proven to be effective over many years for countless practitioners. The chapters in the following section are organized by intention; for each intention are different workings related to each subject because not every spellcaster works in the same way and there is definite strength in variety.

SIX

Protection

I always wondered why there was so much emphasis on spiritual protection. The way people described the need for protection sounded alarmist and frightening to me. Early on, I began to question whether or not magic was a worthwhile pursuit or if I would somehow be attracting endless hordes of evil beings with no way to defend myself against their bloodthirsty attacks. Fortunately, I learned that the reason why protection is emphasized is that by engaging in magical and spiritual practices, a person *does* attract a higher amount of astral attention. Though the attention itself is not necessarily evil, any nonphysical beings that would decide to pay us a visit could be quite disruptive to our lives.

The more positive magic and ritual we practice, the less visible we become to negative entities because we maintain a presence on the upper half of the spiritual polarity. Just as it is harder for someone on the street to clearly see somebody looking out a window on the thirtieth story of a building, so too is it difficult for a negative entity to see someone who resides in the positive spectrum of spirituality. But if this is the case, why the need for protection? For starters, protection is a good precautionary measure against entanglement with any negative entities that may be in the area as well as any other entities whose energy would not be in harmony with the magical goal. As well, there are times when the magic we practice is negative; banishings, bindings, dissolution of obstacles, etc.; at these times, we become more vulnerable to that side of the polarity.

The concern needn't be overwhelming as long as we take the proper protective measures when we do the working and remember to fill in any energy vacuums created by banishing with a blessing of some type to restore equilibrium. The last and most basic reason for protection magic is the need for protection in the physical world. Whether accidents, natural disasters, or dangerous people, there are mundane safety concerns that can be addressed and potentially skirted using magical methods of protection such as amulets, poppets, and ritual work. Far from an alarmist attitude, keeping ourselves safe really should be a priority.

Amulets, Seals, and Sigils

Definitions are a funny thing in magic; one practitioner's definition might not match another's and it can sometimes cause conflict. In truth, a great many pronunciations and definitions vary from one individual or group to another; a good example of this is the word *amulet*. I have seen it defined as a natural charm such as a shell, stone, feather, acorn, or nut that has been charged with a specific nature and carried as a magical article. I have also seen it as another term for a charm, where amulets are either objects enchanted to bring luck or protection. The first definitions I learned (and the ones I still use), were that an amulet is a magical object, natural or created, designed to offer protection to its bearer. Its contrast is a talisman, an object natural or created, magically designed to draw in energy or a goal such as luck, love, prosperity, or healing. The word "charm" is an all-encompassing term referring to any magically charged object. Keeping this in mind, I define a *sigil* as a specially created symbol expressing magical intent such as those inscribed on an amulet and a *seal* as an energetically-created symbol used as a magical protection for a structure or area.

A Sigil for Protection

Sigils are most often created through the use of magic squares, which are numerological devices consisting of rows and columns of numbers that each add up to the same number no matter the direction they are added together. These squares have been made for centuries and are particularly used in ceremonial magic to call upon planetary, "angelic," or "demonic" forces. A good example of a magic square, especially for the purposes of protection is the square of Saturn.

Square of Saturn

In numerology, each letter of the alphabet is assigned a single-digit, numerical equivalent used to determine the number value of the magical intent.

A=1 B=2 C=3 D=4 E=5 F=6 G=7 H=8 I=9
J=1 K=2 L=3 M=4 N=5 O=6 P=7 Q=8 R=9
S=1 T=2 U=3 V=4 W=5 X=6 Y=7 Z=8

For a good protective sigil, write out the word "protection" and use the numerology table to determine the numeric value of the word. The value is "7+9+6+2+5+3+2+9+6+5," that is, "protection" in numbers. Next, draw a small circle on the number 7 box on the square of Saturn to indicate the starting place, then draw a line from the 7 to the 9, then continue on to the 6, 2, 5, 3, 2, 9, 6, and 5. Once you reach the 5, draw another small circle to indicate the end. One last thing, when you add up all of the numbers in "protection," you get 54. In numerology, numbers must always be reduced to a single digit, so we add the 5 and 4 together to get 9, the total numeric equivalent for protection. Mark a small square on the sigil in the 9 box to indicate that this is the "total square," which should give you a Saturn square that looks like this:

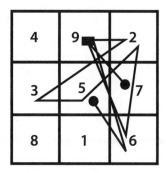

Protection Sigil on Square

If we remove the Saturn Square, we are left with a symbol, the sigil of protection. The sigil can then be engraved on metal or drawn on parchment using black ink and charged with energy to offer protection. Traditionally, the sigil is engraved on one side of an amulet and personal identifying symbols are engraved on the other so that the magical energy is channeled to the proper person.

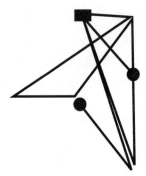

Finished Protection Sigil

Personal symbols can include the person's name written in one of the magical scripts such as runes or ogham, a special magical symbol if you have designed one as a personal sign, your astrological symbol, and so on. Once made, these sigils can be placed anywhere inconspicuously such as the home, car, or carried on the person.

If you wish to carry a less unusual charm of protection than a metal disc or parchment square inscribed with odd, archaic symbols so as not to draw attention or gain a reputation as being odd if they are discovered, an amulet in the form of jewelry can be created that employs the use of the sigil albeit in a more discreet way.

Subtle Protection Amulet

Any jewelry—a ring, pendant, locket, cuff link, tie tack, bracelet—can be transformed into an amulet. Ideally, the article of jewelry should contain iron, gold, (preferably) a black gemstone such as obsidian, jet, or onyx, or show a protective symbol such as a pentagram, hexagram, or cross. Whatever is chosen, cleanse it with blessed salt water, then clean water, and then thoroughly dry it before consecrating.

Items Needed

- Chosen article of jewelry
- Protection sigil drawn on paper
- Black candle
- Protection incense (see page 247)
- Protection oil (see page 247)
- Cup of salt water
- Athame
- Straight pin (optional)

Procedure

After the circle has been cast, carve a pentagram on the black candle using the athame (though many Witches would never use it for actual physical carving), your fingernail, or a pin. After carving, anoint the candle with the Protection oil from both ends to the middle, placing it in a holder on the altar. In front of the candle, set the jewelry on the sigil. Place the cup of salt water to the left and the censer of burning incense to the right. Anoint your wrists, forehead, and the back of the neck with the oil. Light the black candle.

Holding the athame pointed at the jewelry, send and visualize energy being absorbed into the jewelry both from you and from the sigil underneath it. Say the following to seal the spell:

Sigil of power, ignite this spell,
protective force this (name of jewelry) shall bear;
within the charm, energy swells,
keeping me safe whenever I wear.
Orb of security twice the length
of my outstretched arms:
radiate from the amulet
and shield me from harm.

Pick up the jewelry and anoint it with a bit of salt water. Hold it in the smoke of the incense, and pass it over the candle flame to consecrate it in the four elements. Conclude the rite. Wrap the jewelry in black cloth of natural fibers when not in use.

Sealing a Home

Beyond the carrying of amulets, there are other means of protection that, though more involved, offer strong protection without the need to be in continual contact with a charm. For example, to shield a home from danger, we can go from room to room in a clockwise fashion and use the athame to draw energetic pentagrams over each window and door to seal the house. These pentagram seals can be repeated at each full moon if desired to strengthen the charge. Another way to protect the home or any building for that matter is to actually give it a guardian in the form of a poppet.

Protection Poppets

Witches and other magical workers have power, and it can be projected through thoughts, emotions, and actions. Indeed, these forces work in tandem to create magic. The power itself is the spark of life, and it can be used to create a being with a moderately independent life force of its own that can then serve as an astral creature of protection—a "nocturnal servitor" as they are sometimes known. To create this being, a form must first be decided upon, and a physical version of the chosen form must be created out of clay. The exact nature of the task you need the creature to perform must be considered, and the exact life span of the creature must be firmly established.

It is inadvisable to allow these creatures to live longer than a lunar cycle, the usual time span being from one full moon to the next. If left unattended, they can become too powerful and potentially dangerous. Therein lies the reason this ritual is an advanced one—the level of knowledge required and the responsibility and potential spiritual liability the spell caster takes on when performing this magic is too great for the beginner.

Nocturnal Servitor Ritual

These beings are created to be protective in nature. As such, their appearance and demeanor should be intimidating. A turtle, for example, is not as good a choice as the image of a wolf, bat, or some kind of "scary" creature. The creature's fearsome power is one of the primary reasons that they *must* be unmade at the appropriate time. If they are left to linger, they gain more independence and can become disruptive, poltergeist-like things. A good situation in which you would make a poppet for this purpose is a clear cut, specific task such as protecting your home while you are away on a trip.

ITEMS NEEDED
- Black clay image

PROCEDURE
Always hand-write this spell in black ink on a piece of paper, including the timeframe and goal within it. The goal and timeframe must be specific to this working and should be freshly done whenever a creature is created. That is, you cannot repurpose a servitor you made a while ago to a different purpose. Remember to be specific in the nature of the job and the timespan.

An image of the desired form for the creature must be molded out of black clay. It doesn't matter the type of clay; even modern polymer clay works. Once you have a reasonable likeness in the form of the creature, decide on a unique name for the being and which deity you would prefer to call upon in order to bring the creature to life. If you choose not to work with a deity, this rite can still be performed though it will require more personal energy to create the servitor. Whatever your choice, the ritual may begin when you have decided.

Starting the Creature

Cast the circle, invoke the chosen deity, raise power within yourself, and then take the image to each direction and summon the elemental energies into the image. Move in a counterclockwise direction and go to each quarter three times. Once done, take the image to the altar and call to the deity as you visualize the creature coming to life. Say:

> I call on (deity) to aid me in bringing this creature to life!
>
> *(Speaking to the creature):* Having been brought to life by my will and through the power of (deity), I call upon you to complete the task for which you have been created. This task shall be your sole purpose of being and shall be your only thought. All your energies and effort will go to the completion of this task and this task is (name task). You will venture forth to (name destination) and fulfill the goal of (name goal); returning to your physical body when the moon is full once more at which time your life will cease.
>
> I hereby send you forth to fulfill this goal and as I will, so mote it be!

Visualize the astral form of the creature heading off to its destination, and then conclude the rite. Keep the written spell and the clay image in a safe place until you need it to unmake the creature.

Ending the Creature

Re-create the circle and invoke the same deity. Mentally pull the creature back into its physical form. Take the form to each of the four directions, this time moving clockwise, and push the elemental energy of that quarter back out of the creature and into the cosmos. Move through the circle, going to each quarter three times. Once all of the energy is out of the creature, the clay image must be broken and the written spell burned in a cauldron. Once the ashes have completely cooled, empty the ashes and bits of clay into a clean paper bag. Bury the bag of remnants in the ground.

This type of creation doesn't need to be created very often and should only be done with true need, but there is another similar creation that can be made as a long term guardian of a home and property acting as a sentinel that can even be called to guard the ritual circle.

Home Protection Poppet

Here's an easy way to make a home protection poppet.

Items Needed

- 1 cup beeswax
- 1 tablespoon poke root
- 1 tablespoon ivy leaves, dried
- 1 tablespoon periwinkle flowers, dried
- 1 tablespoon sage, dried

- 1 wooden skewer

- 3 iron nails

- Cauldron or pot (to melt the wax)

- Wooden spoon

- Safe work surface

- Bed for the poppet

Procedure

Draw, paint, find, or print a picture of the type of form you would like the poppet to have. The form can be human, animal, or a fantasy creature; the image is mainly important so you can properly visualize the creature as it is made and that you are able to mold a general shape of the form out of the wax. The next step is to make a bed in the form of a small box, ideally with a lid. The bed can be made of wood, clay, cardboard, or whatever is available as long as it is reasonably sturdy and will fit the poppet. Bless the bed and set it with the other ingredients.

To begin, charge the herbs and nails with protective energy and set them aside. Place the wax in the pot and melt it over very low heat, stirring as needed until the wax is completely liquefied. Remove from heat and allow it to begin to cool. Once it has cooled enough to be firm but not hard, stir the herbs into the wax and then scoop the wax into a lump on your work surface. With your hands, mold the wax into the desired shape and then press the nails into the body of the poppet, making sure to seal any holes in the poppet's body made by the nails.

Use the skewer to add any decorative features to the poppet such as eyes, nostrils, a mouth, etc.

Once the features are added, visualize the creature strongly, raise energy, and charge the poppet with your intent. Call it into existence with a name you have chosen, and fill it with your desire that it serve as a protective guardian that keeps out danger. Fix in your mind the desire that as long as the wax body of the poppet exists, so too does its astral self. If the poppet breaks then the astral guardian will die. Greet the creature with joy and place the wax image in its bed. Put the bed in a secret spot where it will not be disturbed, and the guardian will go about its job. If you need its help, simply call it by name.

To unmake the poppet, thank the creature for its help and with reverence, break the wax image. Place it in a pot and melt the wax over low heat while visualizing that the poppet's energy is released into the ether. Once the wax has begun cooling, scrape it out of the pot into a lump and after it has completely cooled, bury the lump in the ground.

Protective Rituals

There are two protective rituals I like to use; the first creates a charm designed to weaken someone who is causing trouble or harm, and the second is a pure ritual for cleansing and personal protection. The first was inspired by the fairy tale of the Princess and the Pea wherein a princess was so delicate that even though she was sleeping on a high stack of mattresses, she was still disturbed to the point of mild injury by the presence of a single pea placed beneath the bottom mattress. With this in mind, I decided to use a similar dynamic to bear down on someone who is willfully harmful or parasitic in nature.

Princess and the Pea Ritual

This rite can be used to magically encapsulate and temporarily disrupt the energy of a person who would seek to cause you strain, stress, or harm. The ritual was devised to be used in those situations where you have no other option than to be around someone that you don't particularly care for and who is one of those people that enjoys causing trouble. Examples of this would be difficult coworkers with whom you have to share space, or unwanted guests in your home such as difficult family members. They may or may not be energy vampires, but if they are, this ritual will block their ability to drain off your vital energy, thus keeping you safe. You will create and use a special charm that will be placed near where the target of the spell will be sitting or standing the majority of the time. If this is not feasible, it can be placed near you so that whenever the person gets close, their energy is dulled and their effect upon you is lessened.

ITEMS NEEDED

- 1 large obsidian stone
- Black candle
- Cup of blessed salt water
- Binding incense (see page 244)
- Athame

Procedure

Within a circle, on the altar, place the cup of saltwater on the left, the candle in the middle, and the incense to the right. Light the candle and incense, and hold the obsidian in your hands while visualizing that it will absorb negativity, draining it away and leaving only positively charged energy. To tailor it to a specific person, visualize them near the stone and that the stone creates an orb; enveloping them in energy which depletes their negativity. When you feel ready, anoint the stone with saltwater, hold it in the smoke of the incense and pass it over the candle flame, charging it with the elements.

Place the stone back on the altar, hold the athame over it, pointing the tip at the obsidian and say, "Charged with earth, air water and fire to absorb negativity and neutralize threat. Polarity reversed, renewed and inspired; imbalance ensnared, harm caught in a net."

Conclude the rite and place the stone in a secure location as soon as possible such as under a sofa, in a drawer or on a shelf.

A ritual that has been in use within the ceremonial magic community and to some extent the Pagan magical community that confers the practitioner with protection and clearing of chaotic energies or negativity is the Lesser Banishing Ritual of the Pentagram (LBRP). This working is a basic preliminary ritual to prepare a space for ceremony and is similar to a circle casting. I have devised a modified version of this rite that may be used anywhere you can have a private moment. If you are in public and suddenly feel the uneasy need for magical protection, this rite can even be performed in a bathroom if necessary.

Witch's Portable LBRP

Here's an easy way to make a Witch's Portable LBRP.

PROCEDURE

Ideally, be able to roughly determine the cardinal directions (a small keychain compass comes in handy) and start facing east.

The Cross

The words in this portion can be said quietly or simply thought in the mind. Touch the forehead and say, "Blessed be the Sky." Touch the solar plexus and say, "Blessed be the Earth." Touch the right shoulder and say, "Blessed be the Father." Touch the left shoulder and say, "Blessed be the Mother." Hold both hands over the heart and say, "In the name of the Mother and the name of the Father; uniting Heavens and Earth, I am blessed!"

The Circle

Trace a "banishing pentagram" in the east with the first and middle fingers of your dominant hand.

Banishing Pentagram

This is the basic banishing pentagram (most specifically, the banishing pentagram of earth) that can be used to neutralize potentially harmful energies. From the eastern pentagram, pivot to the south while tracing a line from the pentagram to the southern point. Form another banishing pentagram in the south and then turn to the west, still continuing the line and trace another pentagram at the western point. Next, turn to the north, tracing the line and then forming a pentagram and finally, trace the line back to the eastern pentagram to complete the circle.

The cross within the circle is a symbol of earth in astrology and in general represents matter, an "x marks the spot" kind of symbol that can be used as a focal point for magical forces. By blessing oneself in the current point in time and then banishing all disharmonious energies, cleansing and protection of the self is achieved. To complete the ritual, once the circle is complete, visualize the equal-armed cross you've placed on yourself as glowing white light and say, "As above and so below; the powers align and balance within me. I am protected and safe." This concludes the rite. The circle doesn't need to be dispersed as you basically carry it with you.

The banishing ritual can be done almost anywhere whenever you intuitively sense danger. Of course, it helps to develop the intuition to as high a degree as possible. A daily meditative training to move through the different states of consciousness and use of exercises such as those in the following chapter are quite useful.

SEVEN

Divination and Psychic Development

Divination is a wonderful practice that enables us to tap into the currents of events so we may determine possible future events if the currents continue unchanged. Psychic development helps to train our own intuition and psychic abilities so that we are better able to receive and interpret astral impulses and translate them from our subconscious mind into our conscious awareness. Development of our extrasensory abilities aids us in the practice of intentionally piercing the veil between the physical and spiritual for the purposes of gaining knowledge and help in decision making.

There are several exercises that can be practiced to enhance our natural psychic abilities and externalize our consciousness at will in a similar fashion as the transplanting of consciousness.

Instead of "becoming" something else, we simply become more of ourselves; we grow beyond our normal limits and extend our senses into the unknown.

Etheric Tendrils

Our etheric energy is incredibly elastic. It can be shaped and formed with mental focus and extended outward in thin filaments to act as psychic sensors that can pick up disturbances before they reach your location. If the negativity has already reached you, first encircle yourself, ideally using the Witches' Portable LBRP (see page 155) to protect yourself while banishing the negativity from your immediate environment and then send out the etheric tendrils to find its source. The tendrils will pass through your circle but you will remain protected from any harmful energies.

To do this working, go into a meditative alpha state using the Rainbow meditation on page 29 if desired. When you are ready, visualize thin rays of energy emanating from your solar plexus region in eight different directions like beams of sunlight in this direction: front, back, left, right, and the midway points between. After sending these out, pull all the other tendrils back, focusing on the remaining one when you feel drawn in a particular direction. Keep following it mentally to the source of the problem. The etheric tendril will give you impressions of what the source of the trouble is, allowing you to combat it, if necessary.

As a fair warning, my advice is to keep any defensive action general, not aimed at anyone in particular in case your psychic impressions are mistaken or incomplete in their scope. For example, if your impression is that someone you know is sending negativity to you intentionally or subconsciously, refrain from any kind of binding or banishing directed at the person until you've done some mundane investigation into the situation. For more on defensive magic, see chapter 12. It is unwise to outright accuse someone of hexing you or something, so be on alert for odd behavior from anyone you would suspect. Above all, please keep in mind that things such as curses and hexes are very rare.

A more pleasant use for the etheric tendril technique is to send them out to check in with loved ones to make sure they are safe. Using tendrils is less intrusive than astral projection since the impressions one receives from tendrils are empathic in nature (it's not like you're spying on them over their shoulder or standing in the room). To do this, you can send out a single etheric thread directed toward a loved one or send out many, each directed to someone different. The impressions received from several at once can be difficult to interpret and can even induce anxiety, so it is best to start small and work your way up if desired. It is generally considered unethical to do anything more than check in and leave; doing so respects the line between ensuring someone is safe and violating personal privacy. With that in mind, we move from the realm of feeling distant impressions to actually seeing them.

Remote Viewing

The talent to mentally travel to a distant place and gain visual insight as to what the place looks like and what may be going on there, can be acquired with careful training. To begin experimenting with this technique, first choose a place that is easily accessible but that you have not yet been to before; a random store in a mall is a good option as long as you have an idea of its specific location. The reason for choosing a public place is so that you can go there afterward to confirm your impressions as this builds the skill.

To begin, settle into a comfortable chair or sit on the floor and go into a meditative state. When you are ready, visualize the front of the location you've chosen. In your mind, see yourself standing in front of the location. Look around the outside and make a mental note of anything that strikes you as particularly significant. Go inside, and once you're there, look around and psychically browse the place. Observe the layout of the place and make mental note of where tables, chairs, counters, and other things are placed. Conduct a thorough walkthrough in your mind of the location and once you feel satisfied that you have a clear impression of the place, leave the location and return to yourself. Come out of the meditation and journal your impressions of the location.

It's a good idea to repeat this exercise at least three times before actually visiting the location so you will have multiple impressions from which you can build a general feel of the place. When you are remote viewing be sure to avoid the tendency to force an impression or assumption of what you "should" see. Allow the images to form on their own. If the visions change between remote visits, make note of them and compare with the reality when you finally make a visit to the real world store. If you are not totally accurate in your impression, don't despair—it takes practice to perfect these skills. Acknowledge your correct impressions and know that no one can be 100 percent accurate all the time. Pick a new location and repeat the process. It gets easier the more you practice, and once the basic process is achieved to around 50 percent accuracy, you can move on to new exercises.

A more advanced exercise requires a willing partner at a different location but one that is known to you. Prearrange a time for the exercise to begin when both you and the partner can be available and also tell them to perform a unique task or have an unusual object to hold during the exercise but don't let them give you any hint of what it might be. When it is time, go into the meditative state as usual and then mentally travel to the agreed upon location. Note your impressions and see if you can determine what the object or task is and then return to yourself. After you come out of the meditation, journal your impressions and call or visit your partner. Compare your notes and see if you were accurate in any of your impressions. Acknowledge your correct impressions and repeat this exercise whenever desired. After proficiency in this is achieved to at least 50 percent accuracy, move on to the next exercise.

The final exercise also involves a willing partner, but this time the partner is to go to a location unknown to you at a specified time. When the time approaches, go into a meditative state and think of your partner. Focus on the person until you see them in your mind's eye. After you feel the link has been established and you have a clear impression in your mind, try to observe their environment and make mental note of what you see. Even if you cannot quite figure out where your partner is at the time, it will be good to compare notes with your partner afterward to see how accurate your assessment of their surrounds was and whether you were tuning into them. It may help if the person wears a bright color but does not tell you what it is; this will give a strong impression, and if you see the color properly, it is a very good sign that you were tuning into them at the location, not imagining them. If they were wearing vibrant red but you saw pale blue, for example, it was probably more imagination than remote viewing. Practice, practice, practice. Use new locations and colors each time, and the skill will build and progress. Each session should go no longer than thirty minutes to one hour to avoid excessive fatigue.

Learning to see far off places, people, and events within the mind is an interesting and valuable skill, but it is not the only way to see. Outside tools of focus are also used to tap the psychic sense and call forth outside energies, and one of my favorite tools is the special Witch's mirror.

The Mirror as a Portal

The Witch's Mirror is a powerful tool that can not only be used in scrying (the magical art of gazing into a reflective surface for divinatory purposes), but also as a channel for receiving and sending of magical energy and as a portal in which to glimpse the Otherworld. When properly prepared, the mirror becomes a focal point through which energies are drawn and this means that through it we have access to a wide range of nonphysical realities and psychic phenomena. Also known as a magic mirror or black mirror, the Witch's mirror is ideally made of glass that is concave (curves inward) painted with a flat black on the underside. The result is a dark, shiny surface for working.

My personal Witch's mirror is a large vintage oval picture frame I modified by turning the curved glass around and painting it so it became a perfect black mirror in a frame. If you are able to find a suitable picture frame with a curved glass or an old glass clock face, these can easily be modified, but magic mirrors are also available for sale in New Age or metaphysical shops locally or online. If your mirror has a frame, try to make sure it opens in the back so you can access the other side of the glass, which will help during consecration and recharging the mirror.

Preparation

To prepare the mirror for initial use, catch the reflection of the full moon in the mirror to charge it with lunar energy. In capturing the light of the moon within the glass, we are implanting the essence of the lunar forces that correspond to psychic abilities and the element of water, both energies that resonate with the mirror and its power. When the moon's reflection can be seen on the glass, visualize the lunar light being absorbed into the mirror in a similar manner as if you were slowly filling a shallow dish with water. Once the mirror feels "full," bring it back to your altar area.

The next step is to consecrate the mirror with an elixir designed to aid its ability to concentrate spiritual forces. A simple elixir can be composed of one pint of water, two tablespoons of chamomile flowers, and one tablespoon of eyebright or mugwort. Bring the water to a near boil and remove from heat. Add the herbs and cover. Allow to steep for about half an hour so it cools as well. Once cooled, strain the liquid, add an equal amount of vodka or vinegar, and charge with the intent that this liquid will concentrate and condense spiritual energy.

Once made, the elixir can be used to consecrate the mirror by anointing the back of the glass either by applying it over the entire painted surface with a soft brush or using a finger to trace a symbol in the middle of the back of the glass. As for symbols, an equal-armed cross within a circle (which aids in convergence of energy), a symbol of the water element, a triangle with the single point down (which helps draw in the energy of psychic activity), or a personal symbol tying the magic directly to you are all good ideas. If you would rather not use an elixir, you can use your own saliva or simply trace a symbol energetically with your finger. Whatever method you choose, it is a good idea to do the same thing every time; repetitive ritual builds the pattern and charges the tool with strength. Declare to yourself that the mirror is charged as a tool of psychic sight, and place it in the frame if it has one. The mirror is now ready for use.

To Use

To gain proficiency in mirror work, try using your breath. Blow on the mirror so it fogs up to imbue it with your energy and train your mind to see images on the glass. As the fog fades, gaze at it and note any symbols which may appear. Another valuable practice is to burn an incense mixture that helps to spark the psychic mind such as equal parts mugwort and wormwood and allow the smoke of the incense to drift in front of the mirror as you gaze at it with relaxed vision. Allow your focus to be pulled into the mirror mentally and let whatever images come appear of their own accord. Most images in the mirror will be symbolic in nature, especially in the early stages of training. As the skill grows, literal events or visions of beings can start to manifest. Not only that, but mental images, sudden feelings of "inner knowing," aromas, sounds, and even voices can all be possible expressions of mirror work. Once the mirror is consecrated, it should be free from any danger, but if any unpleasant or disturbing images should form, pass an athame or wand over the mirror to erase and banish the image.

When mirror gazing, it is best to work in a darkened room lit only by one or two candles. The darkness aids in the ability to tap the psychic mind and also helps to remove peripheral distractions that can pull your focus out of the mirror and ruin the exercise. Place the candles to the rear of the mirror to provide illumination without reflecting in the glass or place one candle in front of the mirror so you are able to see its flame in the mirror. This provides a different type of experience while gazing. You can try experimenting with both methods to see which works best for you as a primary technique and just use the other way for certain tasks.

Even without using actual smoke from incense, it helps to visualize the mirror fogging up and gaze into the concave glass, imagining it as having infinite depth. If the light of a candle is reflecting in the glass, you can gaze at the reflected flame and imagine you are following it; it is leading you through the mirror. This can be done even without the candle: simply visualize a light or soft glow within the darkness of the glass and mentally follow it. Let the mirror draw you in. To help this process, you could also catch sight of your reflection in the glass and be aware of yourself gazing at this reflection, then mentally "switch around" and imaging that you are then the reflected self, looking out *from* the mirror. Don't worry about being trapped inside mentally or otherwise, because the mirror has been properly consecrated to keep out negativity. As with other methods of transplanting of consciousness, focusing on your physical body (thinking about your face or trying to look at your feet) will bring you back to your normal awareness. Placing yourself in the mirror can assist the portal aspect of mirror work.

To use the mirror as a portal, place the candles behind the mirror so the surface is not obscured by their light. Using an athame or a pointed finger, send energy into the mirror, tracing a symbol of invocation such as this invoking pentagram while concentrating on what, where, or who you wish to contact.

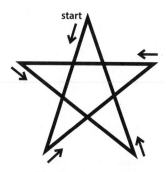

Invoking Pentagram

Relax and maintain an attitude of receptivity being sure to make a mental note of any images or sensations that may form in the mirror. This may take a few attempts, but eventually what you seek will begin to be known.

For using the mirror to aid spell work, you can invoke the destination, subject, or goal of your spell through the mirror using the invoking pentagram, another chosen symbol, or sigil. Sending your energy into the mirror during the projection portion of the spell casting creates a warp effect similar to the mechanism of action of poppets and other sympathetic magic. You can use the mirror during group spell work by passing it around from member to member or have everyone gesture toward the mirror at once, sending their power into it during projection. As a portal, the mirror can concentrate and transmit the power very effectively. Magical energy can also be stored within the mirror for later use. The only difference is that the initial drawing of the invoking symbol is omitted.

You can also use the magic mirror to summon elemental energy. This works particularly well for the element of water, but it can also be done to call each element into a circle casting, assuming you have called the elemental energies within the circle, not outside of it. To do this, hold the mirror facing inward. As you call the element in, visualize its energy is coming through the mirror to manifest into your circle. Repeat the action at each direction; north, east, south, and west. Only calling in the water element through the mirror can be an excellent way to charge it with power right before working with it. If you work with elemental beings or guardians, the western or water being (undines) may be called to aid your working; they work naturally with the mirror and it can be a very effective means of communicating with them.

To Close the Mirror

There are two schools of thought on how a mirror portal should be closed: some believe the mirror is always open so it should be covered with an insulating cloth such as black silk or cotton to stem the flow of energy. Others believe it is best to decharge the mirror and return it to a mundane state after each scrying session or ritual working. Keeping the mirror as an open portal has the benefit of making its use more convenient because it doesn't require reconsecration and empowerment before each use, but it leaves an open energetic entryway into your home. If you forget to insulate it, there is potential for intrusive energies or entities to come through and cause trouble.

Choosing to reconsecrate the mirror before and disempower it after each use has the drawback of being less convenient and practical but is less potentially problematic. If the mirror is disempowered, it doesn't have to be covered and put away after use, it can be left on the altar or hung on the wall. If your choose to keep the mirror active, obtain a large piece of fabric that is either cotton or silk large enough to completely cover both sides of the mirror and bless it with the intent that it will insulate the mirror and contain its energies.

If you would rather disempower the mirror, it is a relatively simple matter. If the mirror was used to call, invite, or invoke energy or an entity, send it away with thanks and cast the banishing pentagram (see page 155) into the mirror to close the portal. Then reverse the steps of the consecration done before the mirror work; retrace the symbol made on the rear of the glass backward from what was initially drawn. To drain away the lunar power, wipe down the front of the glass with a lightly moistened cloth using vinegar, alcohol, or lightly salted water. Finally, dry the mirror with a clean cloth. The disempowerment is complete.

Whether you use the mirror as a tool to connect consciously with your own inner psychic mind or as a portal to invoke or connect with elemental beings or other spiritual entities, this visionary tool can be used to answer questions about magical work you are considering doing in the near future. It can provide sudden inner knowing or counsel from otherworldly beings. Even when other divinatory methods are used, a mirror can be a good idea to include in divination prior to spell work.

Divination Before Spellcasting

If you are thinking of casting a spell that will affect the lives of others, know that whatever you do—even in the person's best interest—may be potentially harmful or controlling. It is a good idea to work divinations to find out beforehand if your spell will be successful and if the result of the spell will be unpleasant or dangerous. This can also be a good idea if you are torn between different courses of action and are unsure which path to take. An example would be difficulty in deciding what type of healing spell to use; is healing through increased strength the way to go or is it better to banish the illness first? Divination is valuable in circumventing any potential misfires or magical backlash.

Whatever your chosen medium—tarot, runes, scrying, or a pendulum—it is a good idea to ask clear questions preferably of a "yes or no" nature and seek general answers. Spending five hours asking about every single aspect and possible choice of potential magical work is unproductive; it can create a dependency on divination and as Ly De Angeles stated in her book *Witchcraft: Theory and Practice*, "this dilutes the powers of psychic aptitude."[6]

---

6 Ly De Angeles, *Witchcraft: Theory and Practice* (St. Paul, MN: Llewellyn Worldwide, 2000), 175–176.

It isn't a sound practice to over-consult oracles, especially for frivolous reasons. Their role lies in their ability to help guide us through difficult times and reveal crucial aspects of our potential futures. If we are too caught up in the idea of knowing what the future holds (as if it is predetermined and cannot be altered), we negate or at least diminish our power to create change. We practically nullify the practice of spell work altogether since at the heart of magical practice is the focus on creating transformation in intentional forms. Now that protection and psychic development have been touched upon, the next step is to reach outward and to initiate change.

EIGHT

Love Magic Taken to the Next Level

One of the primary intentions people focus on when learning to use magic is finding love. Despite the fact that there are tens of thousands of "love spells" readily available in books and on the Internet, it is not as easily done as it looks. In fact, let's be honest here: there is a lot of messed up love magic floating around online and in some books. A great deal of these "love spells" fail to work or even when they do, fail to last for very long. Why? There are important reasons for these occurrences.

Real Love versus Magical Illusion

When a love spell involves a specific target, it is destined for trouble. No matter the wording, all "make her/him love me" type of spells have the effect (when successful) of binding the will of the target to make them have feelings for the spell caster. Aside from the potential magical rebound that may come to the spell caster, another troublesome aspect of such magic is the type of relationship its successful use would manifest. As living beings, we all have subconscious and psychic shielding that protects us from the energies and influence of others. Basically, shielding is like a mental partition that keeps our personal identities intact which is necessary because all beings are spiritually interconnected.

The actual goal of a target-specific love spell is abandonment of individuality. Because of our natural shields, a spell caster would have to use a great deal of energy to break through and dominate a target's will. In any other interaction, this level of dominance could be seen as disturbing or even abusive; magical practice really is no exception. The target would be subconsciously aware of being manipulated in this way, and eventually the relationship would sour because of the conflict that naturally develops as a consequence. So, whether or not a spell caster has personal ethical objections to the use of such magic is secondary to the fact that this form of working is not conducive to a genuine and successful relationship. This type of magic merely creates an illusion of love that will crumble when tested by reality.

Real love magic is about attraction, drawing in the truly compatible so that nature can take its course, mutual feelings can develop, and love can blossom. Attracting those who are compatible with you is not dominance or manipulation of another person's free will; it is merely shifting the patterns of activity so that circumstances arise to bring yourself into contact with those people. In practice, a decent love spell does not really work on a person at all, only situations. The love that may develop as a result is all natural and real; this is the type of love magic that can bring lasting relationships grounded in reality.

Before any magic is used and any love spell is cast, the spell caster must address three issues: their personal concept of love, their self-esteem, and the nature of compatibility. Having the proper mental mindset to be ready to sustain love when it makes itself known is key in having a long term relationship; love spells can bring all the compatible people in the world, but if the spell caster isn't ready to receive love, a solid relationship is unlikely to result.

What Is Love?

It is important to examine your own definition of love. What does a "successful relationship" mean to you? How do you define romance? What qualities do you envision an ideal partner to possess? Is being taken care of an important aspect of what you want in a relationship? Is being a caretaker, provider, or being needed an important aspect? How big a role does your religion play in a love match? Does the other person have to have the same faith as you to be a potential match? These are just some of the important questions that need to be asked and answered within your own mind to develop a proper sense of love's meaning to you.

As harsh as it sounds, there are many, many people in the world who have no idea what love means to them and as a

result are in constant romantic turmoil moving from one partner to the next and being forever disappointed that these partners never live up to the fantasy they use as a crutch. A cursory
glance of almost any daytime talk show is all that's needed to
confirm this statement. Please don't get me wrong: most of the
people on these shows are usually liars, cheaters, or worse—sex
or gender do not seem to be relevant. Liars and cheaters come in
all forms and their behaviors are a big part of the problem, but
no one person can permanently change the nature of another.
Sometimes the only thing we can do to save ourselves is leave.

Speaking in philosophical and magical terms, a lack of focus
and understanding of what love means coupled with a lack of
clearly defined boundaries, low self-esteem, and a fantasy mindset seem to be the reason some people tend to only attract "creeps
and users." If energy is unfocused and our outlook is gloomy, our
polarity hovers around the lower end of the spectrum, serving to
only attract people of this type. This is not to "blame the victim"
for what someone does to them (I hate it when people try to do
that), but merely to identify the conditions that can keep a person stuck and the means to lift out of this energetic booby trap.
As previously stated, the first step is to clearly define what love
means to you and what you want out of a relationship, but also
what you're willing to give a potential partner.

As an example, if you want someone who is college edu-
cated, funny, physically attractive, health conscious, vegetarian, Pagan, between the ages of thirty and forty-five, tall, open
minded, loves comedies, wants children, and has a steady job

making at least $30,000 per year, set that as your intention and do not settle for less. If you want a potential partner to always treat you as the number one person in their life, shower you with affection, and make you feel like royalty, then make this part of you intention as well. The balance for this is that you must also be clear about what you wish to give back; a one-sided relationship is doomed to fail.

Too many love spells tend to focus on the qualities you wish the partner to possess and not enough on what you as a spell caster can contribute. Not to say that these spells are bad, only to say that it is important to keep in mind that love is about both people. If you are willing to take care of a partner when they are sick, support them in times of crisis, shoulder burdens in equal measure, and so on, make this part of your love intention too.

Being clear about ideas and intention related to love strengthens our will and automatically helps move us out of range for the less compatible people. If you won't settle for less, then eventually "less" will stop trying to get your attention. This is not to say that an extensive list has to be written out on paper (though it's not a bad idea), but even giving thought to your intentions will bring clarity and new strength. The next step is to examine the level of self-esteem.

Self-Esteem

This is one of the most vital qualities to possess not only when pursuing love but in every other aspect of life and magical practice. After all, it is very difficult to manifest the will if you do not subconsciously feel worthy of the result. With a strong sense of self-worth, a person can find the strength to refuse to settle, end a dissatisfying relationship, or end a negative cycle forever. Without high self-esteem, the likelihood of putting up with a partner who treats you poorly is much higher; if someone doesn't feel worthy of happiness, the only thing left is unhappiness. Building up self-esteem (if it is low) along with having a clear intention regarding love, is an excellent means to raise the spiritual vibration above those who would likely prey on others for their own gain. It's all about raising polarity up toward the positive pole so that the energy will radiate at the level that corresponds with ideal potential partners. Then later, in spell work, the energy and intention will be projected outward, vibrating in the appropriate rhythm so it will attract the correct people.

Proper self-care and esteem are crucial to any endeavor. If you are worried that your self-esteem may be a bit low, here is a meditative exercise that strengthens it.

Elements of Self-Esteem Ritual

Here's an easy way to boost your self-esteem.

Items Needed

- 6 pink candles

- 1 piece of rose quartz

- 1 small freestanding mirror
  (a regular mirror, not a black mirror)

- Censer with incense charcoal

- Chalice of pure water
- A simple incense composed of equal parts
  dried rose petals and dried chamomile flowers

Procedure

Place the mirror on the altar and the rose quartz in front of it to the right. Set one pink candle on either side of the mirror. The other four pink candles should be used as point candles; one for each of the cardinal directions. Place the censer behind the mirror and the chalice in front of the mirror, on the left. Cast a circle and settle in front of the altar so that you can see your reflection in front of the mirror. Charge the mirror with your desire for heightened self-esteem and charge the water in the chalice with the same intent. Charge the pink candles on the altar and the incense with the same intent as well.

Light the candles and incense and gaze into the mirror. Pick up the quartz, hold it in your receptive hand (left, if right handed), and relax. Say to your reflection in the mirror, "I love you and you deserve endless happiness and love." Close your eyes and go into a meditation. When you are ready, visualize the circle being filled with bright pink light. This light is emanating from the candles and completely enveloping you. See this light as charging your body and the rose quartz with the loving energy of pure self-esteem. Feel in tune with the universe, that all of creation is in harmony with you. Allow the feelings of love and harmony to touch your soul. Bask in this feeling for as long as desired and then when you wish to end the ritual, mentally push any excess pink light into the rose quartz, keeping what you need and creating a charm out of the stone at the same time.

When ready, come up out of the meditation and once again say, "I love you and you deserve endless happiness and love" to your reflection in the mirror. To seal the charge into the stone, hold it briefly over the right pink candle, in the smoke of the incense and anoint it with a few drops of the water while saying, "Dissolving self-doubt and unwarranted fear, creature of earth, touched by fire, water and air; radiate self-esteem to those who come near, increasing our power of love to share." Finally, snuff out the candles and open the circle. Ideally, the mirror and rose quartz could be placed on a bedside table so that it can be seen upon waking each day. The "I love you" affirmation can be repeated each day and the quartz carried as a charm if desired.

Importance of Compatibility

Have you ever noticed that a lot of relationship-related self-help books seem to be offering strategies to help keep people together despite the fact that they are fundamentally incompatible? I have seen books, articles, and advice columns written on how a person can cope with a cheater or a mate who doesn't listen or seem to even care. The givers of advice frequently advocate things like trying to focus on the problem person's interests and becoming very devoted to his or her needs…as if the reader is the problem. In truth, it's often that a bad relationship stems from a fundamental incompatibility between the two people that has gone ignored.

Sometimes, especially early on in a relationship, subtle signs are ignored or laughed off as inconsequential or a joke or because of the belief that the person's habits can be changed. This is rarely true. All too often the person who "needs" to change ends up staying the same, and the other person is the one that ends up changing. The truth of the matter is that people show you who they really are by their humor and behavior. It is also true that when someone meets "the one," they know it. Something clicks in the brain, a recognizing of a compatible spirit, and doubts go away. These are the stories wherein somebody says, "I knew he was the one the instant I laid eyes on him" or "when I heard her laugh I knew I was going to marry her." It's not necessarily love at first sight but is always a powerful experience.

Now, I don't mean to imply that relationships cannot be had with those who fail to inspire the love-at-first-sight feeling; as long as two people are relatively compatible and do not diminish each other's happiness, harmony can be found. My personal insight is that when someone is right for you, you know it. All those stories on TV where a guy says, "I have feelings for her" but he's cheating on her are the result of two things: he knows that she's not "the one" for him, and he's too much of a jerk to break up with her before moving on to someone new. And while we're on the subject, my example is not concrete; anyone can be a jerk. I'm not trashing men. To avoid these types of situations, clear intent and self-esteem must be developed and also the desire for a compatible partner.

When performing love magic, some people are so smitten with the type of person they want, they do not stop and consider if they would really be happy with that dream person in their lives. To offset potential problems, the desire for a "correct" love to be drawn to you is a worthwhile goal. Compatibility is more than just being able to get along with someone; it is the Law of Correspondence at work in our lives. When there is compatibility, there is understanding and the potential for true love. Have you ever seen a couple that doesn't actually seem to get along? They say things like "I love you; I don't have to like you," or "We've been married for twenty years and I still don't understand him." These are not statements denoting a high level of compatibility or joy! But compatibility is not about shared interests, the same religion, or anything like that. It is about a shared perception of reality; a similar inner nature that cannot really be expressed easily in words. Please note that different interests or personality types does not automatically mean incompatibility. Opposites can attract and have lasting relationships, but fundamentally incompatible people will never be happy together. If you seek what is correct for you, a compatible person who meets your concept of love and with whom you have a strong connection, the relationship that can form is one of joy, love, and trust. This type of relationship has the greatest chance of success.

Soul Mates

Did you notice how earlier in this chapter, I put "the one" in quotes when referring to a potential partner? I did that because a lot of people have a sense that there is only one person for every-body, a soul mate they are destined to find. If they do not find their soul mate for some reason, true love will forever elude that person. This, like so many other magic-related topics, is one that has many divergent views. Some believe a soul mate is that per-fect, compatible mate, unmatched by any other person. Another view is that soul mates are the group of souls we incarnate with in each life (you must accept the idea of reincarnation for this view to work, of course) and that the relationships we have with them can change from life to life; sometimes they're relatives, some-times friends, enemies, and sometimes love interests, depending on the lifetime. Another view is that "soul mate" is merely a term that we choose to apply to a love with whom we share a profound connection and a deep understanding.

Regardless of your view on soul mates, the idea of seeking a correct partner fits perfectly into each of the aforementioned possibilities. The following spell and potential modifications constitute a projection of a powerful intent designed to bring forth a compatible love.

Elemental Love Spell

This rite takes four days to complete and should be begun during the waxing moon, culminating on the full moon.

ITEMS NEEDED

- Love potion (see page 246)
- Love incense (see page 245)

- Love oil (see page 245)

- 5 pink candles

- Paper and pen

- Chalice of water or wine

- Pentacle

- Athame

- Censer

- Cauldron

- Wand

- 18-inch length of pink cord (natural fiber)

- Rose quartz

- Trowel or small shovel

PROCEDURE
Night 1: Fire and Intention

Anoint the candles with the Love oil while charging them with your desire to find a correct love. Place one candle at each cardinal direction, and place the fifth one on the altar in the middle in front of the cauldron. Light the candles and cast a circle. Envision each of the candles glowing with pink light, aligning your circle with the energies of love. On the paper, write out a list of qualities that you want your partner to possess, keeping it limited to only the most important ones so as not to slow down the process while concentrating on the feeling that you want to have when you are with your new love. Infuse this feeling into the paper. When you are ready, light the paper in the flame of the central pink candle and drop it in the cauldron to burn to ashes. After this, end the rite, extinguish the candles, and open the circle.

Night 2: Air and Communication

Return to the altar, relight the candles, and cast the circle. Light the incense in the censer so that your communication will be carried outward by the smoke. This night is when the spell is refined depending on the nature of your desire. If the union sought is heterosexual in nature then the wine blessing should be done. If the union you seek is homosexual, one of two ritual actions should be done instead: for lesbians, the pentacle charge of the wine; for gay men, the binding of the wand and athame.

Wine Blessing

Holding the chalice in your receptive hand and the athame in your strong hand, lower the tip of the athame into the cup of wine sending energy through the knife and into the wine saying, "As the athame is to the male, so the chalice is to the female and conjoined they bring blessed love." Take a sip of the wine (or water), knowing that as you drink you are taking the love energy into your being.

Pentacle Charge of the Wine

Set the chalice of wine upon the pentacle and hold both hands over it, willing your energy to go into the liquid while saying, "Sacred earth and water pure, shall merge together and new love ensure." Drink a sip of the wine or water, thereby taking into yourself the energy of love. Please note that "water" in the chant refers to the water element symbolized by the chalice, even if you use wine.

Binding of the Wand and Athame

Hold the wand and athame points up, in your strong hand and slowly wrap them with the pink cord while saying, "Air and fire here combine to bring new love that shall be mine." When the cord is almost completely wrapped around the wand and athame, tie a knot in the ends, making sure that the cord is loose enough to slip off the tools (you will do this later) without untying the knot. Kiss the tip of the wand and athame to imbue yourself with the love energy.

After the ritual action, pour the incense charcoal into the cauldron on top of the ashes from the first day and allow it to burn out. Extinguish the candles, end the rite, and open the circle.

Night 3: Water and Feeling

This is the night for brewing the potion. Combine all the ingredients in a glass or enamel pot and simmer for ten minutes. Allow to cool and charge with your desire for a correct love. Once cooled, strain into a container and take into the circle. Cast the circle once again, and sprinkle a bit of the potion in a clockwise circle around you while focusing on how you want to feel when in the new relationship. Afterward, pour the remainder of the potion into the cauldron so that it mixes with the ashes and charcoal. After this, extinguish the candles, end the rite, and open the circle.

Night 4: Earth and Release

On this final night of the spell, return to the circle one last time. After the circle is cast and the candles are lit, take the pink cord (if not already in use) and while focusing on the intent for love, tie three knots in the cord; one at each end and one in the middle, declaring that you are forming a physical representation of your desire. The cord itself represents the physical, and each knot represents the mental, emotional, and spiritual connection you are seeking. If the cord was used to bind the wand and athame, carefully slide it off of them, keeping the knot intact and tying one more in the middle (the ends tied together are the other two knots).

Next, place the cord into the cauldron and end the rite. Once the candles are extinguished and the circle opened, take the cauldron outside. Using the trowel, dig a shallow hole in which to bury the cauldron's contents. Ideally, this hole can be under a tree such as a willow, but even a corner of the yard that has some grass growing over it will be fine. If you do not have access to a yard, a flower pot can be used. Make sure the pot is large enough to hold the dirt, the liquid from the cauldron, and a small herb such as marjoram. Wherever you have dug the hole, pour out the contents—liquid, ashes, and cord—into the earth, releasing the energy of the spell while saying, "Fire, air, water, and earth. Through each element I've sent my spell seeking a love correct for me; by free will and for good of all, new love manifest, so mote it be!"

Cover the hole with dirt and allow the spell to do its work. If you have used the flower pot method, it is a good idea to plant an edible herb that corresponds to love such as basil, marjoram or oregano. In this way, you can grow a magically charged love herb that can be used in recipes to promote love and happiness. Though this spell is complicated, it serves to address each element on its own terms as well as to combine thought, emotion and the power of will crucial to achieving your goals.

Ethics of Lust Magic

Though this chapter is primarily focused on gaining lasting love, it isn't everyone's preferred situation; sometimes we just want to enjoy being single, dating, playing the field, and need a little magical assistance. There really isn't anything wrong with more casual encounters as long as a sense of responsibility and honor is maintained. It is wise to remember that the notion of "what goes around comes back around" is more than a colorful expression; it is part of the natural law of cause and effect. It is also good to keep in mind that magic does not afford someone a free pass for unscrupulous behavior. Magical ethics are always a huge topic of debate, but for me it comes down to common sense; if you wouldn't do the real world equivalent, don't do the magical version.

As an example, if you were a medical professional and you saw someone clutch their chest and collapse unconscious to the floor in a bar, it would be a sensible action to help them and perhaps administer CPR, even without the knowledge or consent since it is an emergency—this has a magical equivalent in some healing spells. There are times when permission cannot be obtained but that shouldn't necessarily be an impediment to action. Conversely under the heading of lust, upon seeing someone in a bar, it is never sensible or ethical to spike their drink to press your advances on them; this has magical equivalent in coercive spells designed to force a specific person to fall in love or lust with the spell caster. In both the real world and magical examples the intent is the same and the level of disregard of another person's feelings and sovereignty is the same. Fully accepting the power and reality of magic means that it should not be considered in any way less than physical action; if magic is real in your life, it's real, no excuses.

If lust-related magic is done toward a specific individual, it (above any other type of spell) must include an "according to free will" caveat in the intention to avoid coercion. The spell is actually more of an attention-grabbing device; if the target of the spell rejects the call, then it has no effect. This type of magic should not be used on specific people without great care. Just because there are ethical considerations, it does not mean that there isn't room for a good lust spell or two in a magical repertoire. Attraction is the key element in any spell designed to draw in potential sexual partners, so instead of casting a spell on someone else, we actually need to cast one on ourselves; creating an irresistible aura that brings in the desired attention.

Seductive Energy Boost

If the wish is spontaneous or general, such as simply seeking to be more intriguing and desirable to potential partners, the appropriate attraction oil (which can be found on pages 243–244) can be dabbed on the wrists, back of the neck, and a little dot on the third eye in order to create a more seductive vibration around the wearer. This is a great simple option that is easy to apply and easy to undo; a simple shower and the spell is broken. If the goal is more specific, the following spell can be used.

Aura of Attraction

This is a simple meditative spell designed to draw in compatible partners.

Items Needed

- Paper and pen
- Attraction oil (pages 243–244)
- 2 red candles

Procedure

On the piece of paper, write out a list of qualities you want potential mates to possess. Because the goal is most likely a short term romance, physical attributes are probably more relevant than intangible personality traits. After the list is complete, cast a circle and anoint the red candles with the appropriate attraction oil (to attract men or women, depending) and also anoint the corners of the list. Light the candles and close your eyes while holding the list.

Visualize meeting new people and see the type of person you want to attract. Feel as though they are drawn to you like a magnet. In your mind's eye, see yourself surrounded by a magnetic red aura that makes you irresistible. Remember to conjure up the way you want to feel when the magic is successful during this visualization. Once you feel the energy reach its peak, say the following to seal the spell, "Drawn to me like moths to flame, I seek only those who kindle my fire; seduction and passion are my aim, sensual pleasure is my desire. By free will, with harm to none, so I say the spell is done."

Fold the list into a little square packet, making each fold toward you, open the circle, and end the rite. As soon as possible, place the paper into your wallet or purse where it cannot be easily seen. The paper will act as a charm to keep the power of the spell around you. Once your goal is reached, the paper can be burned to release the energy of the spell.

NINE

Money Magic Taken to the Next Level

There are a lot of money spells; tons of them, everywhere. Along with love magic, the desire for financial increase is a major magical goal. Spells for this purpose can be found in many books of magic and all over the Internet; a great many of them work with at least an adequate degree of success. But the trouble with money magic is twofold: money is an artificial construct and has basically no spiritual energy, and some practitioners have a mindset about money that ends up being counterproductive to success. It is just as important to have a proper level of self-esteem when working for money as it is when working for love. If we subconsciously feel undeserving of prosperity, our magic will be significantly hampered by this belief.

On the other end of the self-esteem spectrum, it is wise to avoid being greedy, believing that endless riches should be yours. Balance is a key to prosperity consciousness. It is important to be conscious of the nature of abundance (and deficiency) so that an equilibrium can be maintained within the polarity of extreme poverty and ostentatious wealth. Money should never become the focus of existence, as it distracts a person from genuine fulfillment in life, but it is sensible to want enough money to meet your needs. Having to constantly worry about money only serves to distract us from living a productive and fulfilled life even more so than having "too much" money. The polarity of abundance is not really about having too much or too little wealth, but instead wealth versus other pursuits relating to spirituality, family, romance, and personal growth. Either extreme is hypothetically of equal disadvantage but let's be honest, being broke is much harder on a person than being rich!

The ideal we should strive for is somewhere in the middle, the calm center where needs are met and the correct amount of money comes with regularity. I'm speaking of course about using magic to bring opportunities and situations in which to earn or obtain money (in such a way as will not cause harm or lack to another) and not about making money appear out of thin air. Some people are afraid of using magic to bring them money, fearing that it may manifest as a result of some tragic occurrence in the form of a life insurance payout or inheritance. This fear is not unfounded; such outcomes are possible because magic takes the most direct route of manifestation.

The workaround to avoid tragedy is stating that as long as the stated conditions for the magic preclude any negative occurrence, the "most direct route of manifestation" must by necessity avoid any unpleasant possibilities.

Giving to Receive

In most spiritual traditions, it is considered bad to only do nice or helpful things in order to get something in return. It is usually thought to be selfish and manipulative in nature and perpetuates a cycle of dysfunction and calculated transaction that only feeds itself. I do not recommend this type of giving to receive. Granted, it is a difficult balance to strike that a person mustn't *expect* to get something in return when they give something, but at the same time, *set the intention* that what they give out will benefit everyone, including them. A fundamental principle of prosperity magic is to cultivate a mindset of conscious gratitude and (perhaps paradoxically) the ability to give freely.

Intentional gratitude for what you already have is said to build the foundation for future prosperity. The ability to freely give reinforces our connection to all things and helps us avoid being too self-centered or greedy and helps to keep our polarity relating to abundance on the higher end of the spectrum. A word of caution regarding giving is appropriate here: never "give 'til it hurts" if you can help it—really, it's as imbalanced as not giving at all. If we give away all of our resources, we have nothing left to take care of our own needs and are therefore harming ourselves. Giving in this way not only serves to diminish our present prosperity but also breaks down the current of energy that would ensure future abundance and financial security. The reason for this is that if your pattern of behavior is to leave ourselves weakened, destitute, or unprotected, then that is the energy we project. Self-care in all of its mental, physical, emotional, and magical forms is important not only for prosperity magic but for positive well being in every aspect of life.

Long Term Abundance

In order to cultivate a life of general financial prosperity, it is important to focus on the magical energies relating to money. Because money is artificial, it doesn't have any inherent power. Money is a symbol, and what it symbolizes are the forces of expansion, growth, abundance, and increase. These are universal and natural tendencies mirrored in the fertility of nature; the fruit ripe on the trees, plants heavy with vegetables, and fields of flowers in bloom—each are expressions of a similar energy. Beyond any earthly examples of growth, the energy of Jupiter is attuned to good fortune, expansion, and prosperity and can be called upon in any money magic for a power boost. The planet Venus is attuned not only to love but also fertility and growth, and it too can be called upon for money magic. Given the vital place the sun holds—the literal center of our solar system—its energy corresponds to abundance and success which are perfect for money spells.

A simple example of harnessing these planetary and solar energies in money magic is creating an herbal charm bag consisting of herbs associated with Jupiter such as sage, cinquefoil, and cloves mixed with herbs attuned to the Sun such as heliotrope, chamomile, and cinnamon tied into a pouch made from green or copper colored fabric for the influence of Venus. The bag can be charged and either carried on the person or stored in a place where the wallet or purse is kept or also where any important financial documents are stored. Charms radiate their influence around their immediate environment and can increase opportunities around a person by making them more entrancing, surrounding them with an appealing aura that sends the signal to others to choose this person over the rest. Quite a number of herbal charms can be created and placed wherever needed. This will help keep your energy and environment attuned to general prosperity. For a specific monetary intent, you can use the following spell.

Prosperity Spell Box

A spell box is a powerful physical representation of your intent. It is a form of sympathetic magic in that we bring together ingredients that correspond to the intent, charge them with the energy of our desire and project this goal outward to bring manifestation of its actual form into our lives. The amount of herbs needed will vary due to the size of the box chosen and can be anywhere from a tablespoon each to over an ounce. Equal proportions are used.

Items Needed

- 1 small box
- Paper and pen

- 1 green candle

- 1 blue candle

- 1 gold (or dark yellow) candle

- Money oil (see page 246)

- Money incense (see page 246)

- 2 lodestones

- Cinquefoil

- Sage

- Heliotrope

- Cinnamon

- Chamomile

- Barley

- Decorations or photographs
  relating to your specific intent

Procedure

Cast a circle and light the incense. Anoint the candles with Money oil, charging the green candle with the energy of Venus and placing to the left on the altar, the blue candle with the energy of Jupiter and setting it in the middle, and the gold candle with the energy of the sun on the right. Light the candles. Charge the cinquefoil and sage with the energy of Jupiter, the heliotrope, cinnamon and chamomile with the energy of the sun and the barley with the energy of Venus. Charge the lodestones to attract money to you like a magnet.

Write out your exact intention on the piece of paper; if you need a specific amount of money for a bill or purchase, write that amount on the paper and what it will be used to do. Fold the corners of the paper toward you to cover what you've written. If the needed money will be used to purchase something, the decorations or photographs can be of that thing or its equivalent. If the money will instead be used to pay a bill, you can use a photo copy of that bill with "Paid in Full" written on it in ink as part of the decoration. To begin filling the spell box, combine the herbs together and sprinkle them on the bottom inside of the box to cover it.

Once the herbs are placed, add the paper with your intent written on it. Cover this with the photograph and/or other decorations and the lodestones. Once the box is fully assembled, hold it in both hands and focus strongly on your magical goal. Visualize the box filled with light; green on the bottom, blue in the center and gold on top, each layered on top of the others. See this box as a magical magnet designed to draw your goal to you. When your visualization is at its peak, you can say the following to seal the spell, "Powers of growth, expansion and success, bring to me what I desire. For good of all with harm to none, prosperity inspire." And then state out loud what you seek and that this box shall remain intact until your goal is reached.

The rite can be concluded, the circle opened, and the spell box secreted away so it will not be disturbed by others or placed in a prominent location where you will see it daily, depending on your living situation and desire. Once your goal is achieved, you can release the energy of the spell box by either burying the contents in the ground or gathering up and burning the herbs in a fireplace or cauldron and cleansing the box and any decorations you want to keep. Passing them through the smoke of burning frankincense is sufficient to cleanse them. It is beneficial to keep the lodestones as prosperity charms which can be carried with you if desired.

TEN

Allies and Helpers

One of the traditional practices associated with Witches and other workers of magic is working with allies; non-human beings whether they are animals or spiritual entities, and employing them in magical work or seeking their aid for decision making or protection. There are, as usual, varying views on the nature of and how to properly work with these allies. They are often called familiars, and I will present a few different possibilities from which to choose. Let's start with what are usually the easiest of potential helpers to contact: animal familiars.

Working with Animal Familiars

In her book *Earth Magic: A Dianic Book of Shadows* (Earth Magic Productions, 1998), author and Witch Marion Weinstein describes animal familiars as equals who are from the animal realm. They are not a Witch's pets but rather coworkers.

Weinstein viewed animal familiars as having a psychic link to the Witch with whom they have a working relationship and believed they were active participants in the Witch's magic. Ly De Angeles expressed a similar viewpoint in *Witchcraft* regarding animal familiars; that they are not pets (even though they may choose to live with you) and will have their own lives separate from you. She also speaks of a psychic connection between familiar and Witch and that they have the ability to come and go from a magic circle without breaking the seal.

De Angeles and Weinstein both write that animal familiars are rather easy to recognize by their behavior; they are able to communicate with the Witch psychically or by making their needs known, and they are also drawn to occult work of all types. Their views on familiars mesh with what I was taught about them; that familiars are special creatures who choose to work with a Witch in a relationship meant to be mutually beneficial, they help us in our magic and provide companionship and in exchange, we give them sustenance, shelter, love, and support. Animal familiars are capable of being messengers, magical partners, sentries, and magical "alarms."

Like most other animals, familiars have the ability to read us and will let you know if something is menacing about an individual that may have slipped past your own intuition. To work with a familiar in the circle is simply a matter of having them present. Even if they are sleeping, it is still considered participation (though if they wake up agitated, it could be a sign of negativity). To help make a decision, write the choices on paper and placed them on either side of the familiar. Next, ask the familiar to go to the best choice. This can also be done with two bowls of food, the bowls being somehow marked with each option.

Another view regarding animal familiars is the idea that any animal can be a familiar because many animals appear to have extrasensory abilities and the majority of pets can form very close relationships with the people who adopt them. Personally, I think it all comes down to personal choice: if you already feel a bond with a pet, you're all set. If not you can send out a call for a familiar. A simple method for doing this is to figure out what type of animal you would like the familiar to be and charge a brown candle with this mental image. It is a good idea to keep your visualization relatively general so as not to eliminate good candidates. Light the candle as you send out a call for "the ideal familiar with which to work, in perfect love, trust, understanding and mutual benefit, for the highest good, so mote it be" or something similar. You can repeat the call at the same time every day to strengthen the call, if desired.

Once the animal makes itself known, a test can be administered by casting a circle and doing a basic devotional to a deity, scrying or tarot work, a self-blessing, etc. Basically, do a simple working that uses magical energy or the psychic senses to determine whether or not the potential familiar is drawn to this work. If it chooses to join you in circle (or stand just out side of it like a guard) and is not intrusive or disruptive, then it is a good choice. If on the other hand, it becomes agitated at the circle, runs out of the room, or enters the space and jumps on the altar and nearly knocks over the candles (use wide heavy pillar candles for the test and keep their number low), or lies right on top of what you are trying to do, the animal is probably not the ideal familiar for you. As long as the animal in question does not cause trouble—again, even if all it does is sleep in the circle—it is still lending its energy and can make a good addition to your magical practice.

Working with Familiar Spirits

Another version of familiars associated with the practices of Witches in the past is that of familiar spirits, beings or aspects of beings from the otherworld such as someone's spirit guides that are in contact with the Witch in a manner similar to mediumship. These "spirits" can also be manifestations of the person's higher self or insight from what is called the collective unconscious. To work with them is to allow the conscious mind to accept communication from their realm. To begin initial communication, it is the safest method to work within a circle, formally is best, but at least the use of the Witches' Portable LBRP on page 155 is recommended. It is a good idea to have a pen and paper in the circle to record impressions.

Once encircled, perhaps in front of an altar lit by a black candle to the left and a white candle to the right to encourage a cyclic motion of energy, go into a meditation to shift consciousness. After the proper mental state is achieved, make a personal statement of intent and welcome, then relax, quiet, and open the mind. Eventually, impressions will come. This practice is similar to scrying except that it is within the mind, and in addition to mental images a type of mental sound can be heard. As it progresses, spirit voice can sound like listening to a television that is on in the next room, i.e., you can hear something but it is difficult to understand or decipher the sound. With continued practice, this jumble of noise should fade into clarity.

Not all messages come through in "vocal" form; many come through as visual images or feelings. For example, after some progress, a question and answer dialogue can be formed. Ask what image or sensation is a "yes" and what image or sensation is a "no." Once these are determined, yes or no questions can be asked for problem solving and growth. Please be advised that working with familiar spirits should be done in moderation, and that not every sensation or mental image is automatically from "the other side." Over the course of regular practice, you will begin to notice a pattern and "feel" to help distinguish between imaginings and communication. It is very important to avoid obsession with this type of working as it is with any spiritual exercise. Always work within a protective circle to avoid negativity and do not use this technique when under great emotional stress; we're not trying to create any mental issues, after all.

Working with spirits can be a wonderfully enlightening experience as long as the proper precautions are taken to avoid negative contact and training does not border on obsession. Don't go to your spirit for every little thing; build a respectful relationship, and its benefits will manifest in the mundane world.

Creating an Astral Familiar

Another type of familiar is one that is not found or contacted, but formed by the spell caster. This creature can be similar to a nocturnal servitor or protection poppet, but it can also be made for general use. Instead of only being created for the length of a moon cycle and for a specific task, an astral familiar can live for many years and be a multipurpose ally. For example, an astral familiar can be created as a circle guardian even from the essence of one of the elements to be a type of personal elemental if calling in the watchtowers or other beings is not desired.

To create an astral familiar, first decide on a unique name for the creature, figure out what form you wish it to take, decide on its exact lifespan, and then choose a physical object to be the familiar's "home." This object can be representative of what you want its astral form to look like such as a gargoyle statue or glass animal, or it can be a general item such as a large crystal or a piece of symbolic jewelry. The home for the being could also be a painting hung on the wall of either an animal or fantasy creature. It is not advised to make this being appear human because they are not human and allowing one-self to believe otherwise can cause problems. Likewise, it's a good idea to refrain from forming an emotional attachment to them. Though an affection can be felt, it is best to equate them to pets of a sort rather than peers or higher beings. Additionally, try to match the form with the element that is going to be used in their creation. A fish, shark, or seagull would make a great deal more sense for a water creature than a mountain goat or a phoenix, which would suit the earth and fire elements respectively.

Once the form is decided upon and a "home" is chosen and/or obtained, form a circle with the home object on the altar and go into a meditation. Once the proper mental state is reached, envision a seemingly endless expanse of the energy of the chosen element surrounding the area. Visualize that the energy begins to condense together, compressing down slowly to form the creature. When the creature feels nearly formed, mentally instill within it, its name, and that it will always return to its home object when its tasks are completed. Assign it its exact date of birth and death and place it into its home. Charge it with as much energy as feels necessary until a sense of completeness is felt. Write down the name, element, date of birth, date of death and home object of the creature so as not to lose track of the important facts about this being.

Once created, the familiar can be immediately sent to complete a task, but please note that once it has completed its task and returns that is when the process of manifestation begins. For example, if the creature is sent to contact a family member and advise them to call you and the familiar goes, transmits the message and returns; that is the beginning of the timeframe to wait for the family member to develop a conscious awareness of a desire to make contact. For larger tasks requiring longer trips, it is a good idea to call the being back to you and recharge it every so often; every couple of days or so.

Working with Elemental Spirits

The essence of each element, the spiritual prototypes of earth, air, water, and fire are the elemental spirits. These beings en-soul their physical counterparts and are the "why" behind the "what" of elemental manifestation. Aside from calling them together in order to protect a magic circle, they can also be called individually for divination work such as calling a water elemental to aid you in crystal scrying or mirror work, an air elemental to help with the mental processing of reading tarot cards, a fire elemental to help with fire scrying, or an earth elemental to help you in deciphering the symbols of geomancy (earth divination), such as interpreting lines and dots randomly drawn in sand or soil. You simply call them in the same manner and proceed with your work. And don't forget to thank and release them when finished.

The more naturally attuned someone is to the element they seek to evoke, the better and closer the working relationship will become. Some of us feel more aligned to one element over the others, at times this may be due to our astrological sign (for example, I'm a Leo and I feel more aligned to the fire element) or it might be due to geographic proximity (growing up near the ocean could give a person a great love of the water element). This is not to say that a person cannot work with each element; if you already have an affinity for a specific element, it will make for a more profound alignment. Many people work successfully with each of the four elements, even if they have a preference for one over the rest. All it takes is time, commitment, and desire; the skills will develop and everything will fall into place.

ELEVEN

Healing

One of the most important uses for the magical arts is the practice of healing. There really is no greater example of transformation than to see vibrant health restored to someone who was stricken with illness. The art of magical healing is a vast spectrum of diverse methods ranging from simple herbal charms that encourage continued good health to large-scale rituals involving a group of people all attuned to the goal of restoring the target's vitality. Needless to say, magical healing should not be used in place of standard medical care, rather as an adjunct to it.

Magical energy is a powerful vitalizing force that can fuel the body to heal itself but illnesses or injuries can sometimes be too great for the body to resolve, thus the need for standard medicine. Both practices can work in tandem; regular medical care could destroy an illness and magical healing could restore the body, for example. Aside from actual healing, magical energy can also be channeled to strengthen the body and help ward off illness, minimize swelling, or repair an injured area. Because healing is frequently done for other people, there are ethical considerations to weigh. Magical ethics in general are a touchy subject with many varied opinions; some are on the extremely relaxed "do whatever you want" end of the spectrum whereas others go all the way to being so restrictive that they practically prevent any magical action being taken at all.

I am of the opinion that if properly done, magic geared toward healing another can be used without their knowledge or permission as long as certain conditions are worked into the spell. For example, some of the concerns I've read that people have with using magic "on people" even in a healing capacity is that it interferes with their free will and potentially any spiritual or karmic lessons they may need to learn from the illness. This can easily be avoided by making sure the intention that the magic be "according to their free will," "only for the highest good," "with harm to none," and/or "for the good of all" be incorporated into the working. These are safeguards that will neutralize the magical effect if the recipient is subconsciously opposed to the work or if the person is meant to be sick to learn a karmic lesson or similar. One or more of these intentions can be added into the spoken words of a spell, as a final statement as the power is being sent, or written on paper along with the healing goal to be carried, hidden, or burned as part of the magic depending on the spell's nature. In this way, healing energy can be sent to someone in need without fear of it having had a harmful or negative effect instead of the help it is intended to bring. I'm not advocating using magic on people without their knowledge or consent as a matter of standard practice; this sort of magic is more for situations where the intended target is not able to give permission due to a lack of consciousness, as one example. My own opinions aside, magical ethics often come down to personal choice; as long as none are harmed, let your conscience be your guide.

As a means of strengthening the body against illness, magically charged food is often a good choice. Since food is already nourishing and strengthening to the body, adding a magical boost to it during cooking or before serving can increase the body's natural defenses against illness and imbalance. Ideally the food would be something you've cooked yourself and healthy. Charging a candy bar with energy doesn't have quite the same effect that an empowered batch of homemade soup, loaf of bread, or cake would, though it is better than nothing.

Charging Food

Imbuing food with healing power or any other type of intention can be done in a variety of ways, singly or in combination. Stirring soup or a sauce with a spoon provides an opportunity to charge it with energy. Focus on the intention and send the energy through the spoon into the food as you stir. Incidentally, make sure to stir it in a clockwise motion to build up the energy. If baking a cake, cookies, or bread, a symbol, rune, or even the words "healing" or "strength" can be traced on the pan with intention and energy after greasing the pan to imbue the food with the magic as it bakes. These simple procedures can also be greatly enhanced. Each ingredient in a recipe can be measured out into bowls and charged separately before combining, words can be spoken silently or out loud, symbols can be cut into loaves or cakes, and ingredients can be arranged to convey intent (pizza toppings work beautifully for this!), and the food itself can be empowered with energy one last time after it is cooked to seal the charge. Using food for its nutritional content and as a means of taking in magical energy is a great supplement to any other heal-ing work or medical treatment a person needs.

Sometimes instead of empowerment or strengthening, a cleansing, releasing, or purging type of energy is called for to get rid of a problem even before any restorative healing magic. It is also a good idea to cleanse the body after doing healing work on others so that any residual illness from their energy field that may have become attached to you is dispelled. A focused ground meditation is a good means of this type of cleansing.

Health Cleansing Exercise

Sit on the ground or in a chair and close your eyes. Relax and visualize astral roots coming from your body reaching down into the earth. Visualize your own aura, and look for any imbalances or negative energy, which can be visualized as dark blobs, green glowing particles, red orbs, among others. Mentally gather and push the negativity down through your body and out through your roots into the earth to be recycled to a higher purpose.

Breathe in and out slowly and evenly. As you do, imagine you are drawing in positive energy through your breath; perhaps you see it as beautiful sparkly air or a healing mist, for example. Once the negativity is fully released from your roots and replaced by the positive energy, mentally pull up your roots and open your eyes.

This exercise can be done whenever needed to restore calm and balance to the body. For help with greater health issues, more complex methods of healing can be employed. Some popular methods of magical healing include healing through laying of hands, healing through the use of a magical link, and healing through a group of peoples' combined power.

Healing Through Touch

The laying of hands is a means of passing therapeutic energy to a recipient directly without an intermediary device such as a poppet or a requirement of transferring the power over a great distance. Before coming into contact with the recipient, spend some time alone and go into a meditation. The Chakra meditation on page 33 is an ideal choice for this work because it vitalizes the body's psychic centers. Only use the opening portion of the meditation prior to healing so that you radiate vital energy. Once you are pulsing with magical force, concentrate on the intention that this energy will bring healing wherever it is sent. Now go to the person to be healed. There are two ways the healing work can be done at this point:

Method 1: Hold both hands directly over the area of the person's body known to be the site of the trouble and with great force of will, project your energy into the person, through their pores to the cause of the problem. Fix in your mind the intent that this energy will restore balance and function to the area and that if needed will renew itself by drawing in universal light until complete healing is achieved.

Method 2: This is more of a health clearance and a good practice to use when trying to rid the body of infection. Hold the hands on either side of the recipient's head and slowly sweep the hands down along the body from the head all the way down to the feet with the intention that the magical energy from your hands is acting as a psychic web, catching and holding any illness and carrying it out of the body. When you reach the feet, shake your hands away from the person so as to fling or throw the illness away from them and break the connection to your own energy field. Repeat these passes seven to thirteen times for a complete session.

Whatever your method, be certain to close the chakras and ground all the excess energy after the session so that any illness does not attach itself to your aura. As a side note, the wearing of charged silver bracelets (at least one on each wrist) can help prevent any ill vibrations from traveling up into your body.

Healing Through Psychic Link or "Witness"

If the person in need of healing is not available to be worked on in person, a poppet or other link to them can be used. If a poppet is created, it can be stuffed with healing herbs such as dried carnation petals, mint leaves, hops, rosemary, and other herbs to give the intention greater focus. If a different type of link is used, such as a watch or piece of jewelry belonging to the person, it can either be anointed with Healing oil, such as the one on page 245 or placed in a charm bag with some of the healing herbs to properly focus intent as long as doing so won't damage the item.

In her book *Power of the Witch*, author and High Priestess Rev. Laurie Cabot discusses the power of color in healing work. She writes that different colors can be used to treat different ailments, stating that emerald or kelly green can be used for general healing, light ice blue can be used to treat pain, and red-orange can be used for critical healing of severe illness or injury such as organ damage.[7] In his vastly influential *Complete Book of Witchcraft*, author and High Priest Raymond Buckland also states that the color green is an excellent healing color; it is neutral and vitalizing; "when in doubt, use green."[8] Using this framework, we can tailor the healing magic to better meet the needs of a recipient.

ITEMS NEEDED

- Psychic link or poppet
- Healing oil (see page 245)
- Healing incense (see page 245)

---

7 Laurie Cabot, *Power of the Witch* (New York: Delta 1989), 258–259.

8 Raymond Buckland, *Buckland's Complete Book of Witchcraft,* (St. Paul, MN: Llewellyn Worldwide, 2002), 271.

- 2 candles in correct color
  (green, light blue or red-orange)

- Wand

- Pentacle

- Chalice of water

Procedure

Cast a circle and anoint the candles with the Healing oil. Hold the poppet or link in the smoke of the incense, anoint it with a few drops of water, hold it above the candle flame, and place it on the pentacle between the two candles. Using the wand, summon energy of the proper color and send it through the wand into the link, filling it with power. Fix in your mind that this force will be transferred directly to the recipient to heal them. When you feel you have done all you can, end the rite, open the circle, and keep the link in a safe place.

Healing Through Group Work

If more than one person is going to be involved in the healing magic, the specific result sought must be explained and understood by each member of the group. The exact nature of the work can vary; one of the previously discussed rites can be used with more participants or the following spell can be used.

Cast a circle. If possible, have a photograph of the person to be healed on the altar. Each participant should gaze at the picture long enough to get a clear image of the person in his or her mind. Everyone in the group should link hands and focus on surrounding the person with light in the proper color (green, light blue, or red-orange) so that vital healing energy is infused into their auras. A chant can be composed tailored to the individual who needs the healing. When the group has reached the peak of energy output, everyone can release the visualization and then ground any excess energy. After this, the rite can be ended and the circle opened.

TWELVE

Defensive Magic

No matter how hard we try to be positive and genuine people, there may be times when we feel the need for defense. In the magical community, defensive magic is a very controversial subject; from disputing what constitutes "defensive" magic all the way to debating its use at all, there's no shortage of passionate opinions along the entire spectrum of this topic. Some practitioners absolutely refuse to do anything even remotely resembling negative magic or cursing. They argue that because what goes around, comes around it is very foolish to use negative magic; the energy that returns will be negative itself. To curse another is to curse oneself and as such should be avoided at all cost.

Those who adhere to this philosophy usually deal with the need for defense in less direct ways than binding, hexing, or even psychic influence. Their approach would be more geared toward protection from negativity and also the art of blessing a negative person away from them; deflecting that person from creating disruption in their lives. There is also another more advanced technique that can be used when an enemy is causing harm, spreading gossip, or even using negative magic against us. It is the technique of using their negativity; the energy that they are sending out toward us, to empower ourselves.

Using Someone's Negativity to Empower Yourself

This working requires a lot of visualization and a specific intent. The goal is to harness the energy aimed at you, shift its polarity to the positive, and channel it toward a goal of your own. The result is that you remove the harmful energy and simultaneously enrich your life.

ITEMS NEEDED

- 4 black candles
- 1 Reversible Action candle in appropriate colors (see following)
- Paper and pen to write your intention

PROCEDURE

A Reversible Action candle has a core of one color and an outer coating of another, and they are usually used to dispel one form of energy while drawing in another. We can also use the candle to transform energy as will be done here. The inner core wax should be in the color appropriate to the new goal and the outer coating should be black. If you cannot find a reversible candle, you can make one relatively easily. Find a candle in the desired color and dip it in melted black wax, or light a new black candle, and drip its wax over the other candle as it melts while holding it over a pan or other safe surface. Once coated and cooled, the candle will be ready for use.

However you obtain a reversible candle, charge it with your magical goal and place it in a holder on the center of the altar over the piece of paper with your goal written on it. Set the four black candles around the circle, one at each direction point. Do not cast a circle for this working, as its natural protective nature makes it difficult to channel the negativity being sent your way. Light each of the point candles and sit before the altar going into a meditative state. Visualize the negative energy you are receiving as being drawn into the point candles and from there, being sent into the reversible candle. After you feel like the candle is "full," pick it up and visualize the energy shifting inward, deeper into the candle, from black into the color of your intent. The energy is being polarized to correspond to the magical goal. When it feels ready, place the candle back on the altar and as it is lit, say the following (or similar) to seal the spell.

> *Sent my way with harmful intent,*
>   *the energy shifts along the plane;*
> *Stripped of negative vibe,*
>   *upward to a higher dimension;*
> *Channeled into my desire,*

what once was loss shall now be gain;
*(**name desire**) for me, now in ascension!*

As the candle burns, visualize the energy streams forth from the candle transformed by your intent out to manifest the goal. When you can no longer sustain the visualization, snuff all the candles in reverse order of lighting to conclude the spell. This ritual can be repeated nightly until the candles are completely burned. The moon phase for this working should correspond to the positive goal, so the waxing or full moon phases are ideal.

As stated earlier, there are differing schools of thought on the subject of defensive magic. Aside from the argument that energy sent out eventually returns to the sender and so any form of negativity should not be used, the other approach is the concept that in order to restore balance to the situation, the sender of harmful intent must receive harmful energy in return. Since there are no guarantees that the eventual energetic return will reach the attacker in a timely fashion, some practitioners believe it necessary to work magic to use a swifter form of justice. The argument for fighting back in equal force to those that would wish us harm is justified and not necessarily subject to the same level of cosmic return as genuine harmful intent. In other words, to curse someone out of hate is evil but to fight back in the same fashion is self-defense.

The bottom line is that it is up to individual practitioners to decide their own magical boundaries. It is incumbent upon every teacher to properly instruct and inform students of the true nature and processes at play in all forms of magic because everyone deserves full information and free choice. Self-defense magic is considered "gray magic" because it employs techniques such as binding, return-to-sender-type spells, and psychic influence, all of which are considered to be manipulative of other people in their process.

Psychic Influence

When someone is creating strong difficulty in your life and there seems to be no other option to get them to stop, psychic influence can be an effective tool to cause the assailant to finally shift focus and find something else to do. The intent must be phrased in a positive manner. If you want them to leave you alone, do not say "leave me alone" but instead something like, "you wish to move to a new city," or "you wish to find a new job," or "you seek new love"—positive ideas that shift the focus. Your stated wish is not necessarily for benevolent reasons but for the simple fact that the subconscious mind more readily accepts influence in this manner.

ITEMS NEEDED

- 1 single terminated clear quartz crystal point
- 1 yellow candle
- Carving tool (straight pin or small knife)
- Persuasion oil (see page 247)
- Persuasion incense (see page 247)
- Picture of the target or a personal item

PROCEDURE

Cast a circle and burn the Persuasion incense. Carve into the yellow candle your specific intent—in this case, what you want the person to do. Charge the candle with your intent and then anoint it with the Persuasion oil. Light the candle. Hold the crystal in your strong hand (right, if right handed) with the point toward the photograph or personal item of the target of the spell. If no such item can be obtained, then point the crystal in their general direction while focusing very strongly on a mental image of them. Gaze at the crystal as you visualize and when the point is reached where a genuine connection to the target is felt, speak your intent directly to them as if they were standing in front of you. Speak with conviction and be certain that your will shall be obeyed. It is done.

Please be advised that attempting to manipulate or influence in this particular manner is best only done for important reasons both for ethical issues and for one more very important consideration that is not often discussed. When we "cast spells on people" we metaphorically pluck the string of the energy web that connects us and make it vibrate to the pattern of our goal. This action of agitation is how our magic is transferred but also strengthens our bond to that person. All beings are interconnected through the cosmic web but a great many of those connections are, for lack of a better term, "dormant" and go unnoticed but when they are activated, they are not only a channel through which we can send, but also a channel through which energies can be sent to us. This is a major reason it is thought better to alter situations rather than to bend others to our will; because doing so creates a vulnerability within ourselves. Magic is wonderful and fun and exciting but also, serious, complicated and carries a responsibility that cannot be dismissed. Magic directed at specific people is best only done after weighing the pros and cons and deciding the risks are worth it.

Elemental Binding Spell

Sometimes a person is intent on spreading chaos and harm. Try though we may to influence them to stop, the person consciously or subconsciously refuses to quit. Beyond the use of psychic influence, another option to get someone who is set on causing harm to change their behavior is through the use of a binding spell. This type of magic can be difficult to perform as it requires a high amount of energy in order to overpower the subconscious shielding of the target. A helpful method of binding is to use elemental energy to create and seal the bond. By calling in an outside energy source for power, our personal reserves are not overly depleted, and the elemental energy adds to the binding's strength immeasurably.

Items Needed

- Cloth poppet doll with needle and black thread
- Oak moss or cotton balls (for stuffing)
- A personal item from the one to be bound
- 1 tablespoon dried loosestrife (aligned with earth)

- 1 tablespoon dried ivy (aligned with water)

- 1 tablespoon dried slippery elm (aligned with air)

- 1 tablespoon dried nettle (aligned with fire)

- Two black candles

- Binding incense (see page 244)

- Binding oil (see page 244)

- Chalice of water

- Pentacle

- Black cord

- Pen and paper

Procedure

Cast a circle, and make sure to call the elemental quarters. Place the pentacle in the middle of the altar. Anoint both black candles with binding oil while visualizing your intent for the target of the spell, i.e., what you want to bind the person from doing. The black candles should be set on the left and right of the pentacle. Write your specific intent on the paper and fold it into a small packet (much like with psychic influence, the intent of the binding must be stated in positive terms for the best effect). Fill the poppet by placing the dried loosestrife in the poppet's legs. You can use oak moss or some cotton to bulk up the stuffing if the poppet is large and also in its arms. Put the ivy in the abdomen area as well as the paper packet. Add the slippery elm into the chest region, and finally put the nettle in the head of the poppet. Sew it shut.

Hold the poppet in both hands. Call to each of the quarters individually to channel its elemental power into the doll. Call to the element of earth: "Power of earth, fill the legs of this poppet so that its feet are grounded in reality." Call to the element of water: "Power of water, fill the center of this poppet that its gut may know the sense of emotion." Call to the element of air: "Power of air, fill the chest of this poppet that it may breathe in the energy of truth." Lastly, call to the element of fire: "Power of fire, fill the head of this poppet that it may have the strength of mind and will that I see fit."

Next, raise energy in the form of white light while concentrating on whom the poppet represents; focus strongly on the spell's target. When you feel the power is at its peak, mentally drive the white light into the poppet and declare, "(name of target), through earth and water, air and fire, your body has been formed. (Name of target) you shall be. All that you are is a part of she/he, (name of target) you are to me" and fix in your mind that this energy will remain in the poppet and meld with the elemental energies in the doll to create a full astral body for it and magical link to the target.

Now that the poppet is made, the binding can commence. Holding the poppet in your weak hand, begin to wrap the cord around the doll mummy-style so it is completely tied up. As you bind the doll, focus strongly on the intent of the spell and repeat what you what the target to do over and over again to the poppet as a clear order. When the cord is completely wrapped around the poppet, tie the ends of the cord together completing the binding. End the rite and open the circle. Afterward, wrap the bound poppet in natural cloth and hide it somewhere it won't be disturbed.

The Curse of Clarity

Sometimes when a harmful person is unrelenting in perpetuating their dysfunction, inflicting distress upon those around them, the best magical option is to use a spell to bring the full force of understanding of the turmoil the person has caused into their conscious awareness. This is similar in effect to the "Witch's curse," popularized by late author and Witch, Dr. Leo Martello. It goes like this: "I wish you on yourself."

The working itself is simple enough. It is a modification of a standard shielding exercise wherein the person surrounds themselves in an energetic egg of mirrors to reflect back any negativity directed toward them.

If possible, have a personal item for the target of the spell or you can use a poppet made according to the method in the elemental binding spell. Hold the chosen object and focus on the target. See in your mind's eye that they are surrounded by an energetic egg, but unlike a shield, this egg will be mirrored on the inside. Visualize that not only will the energy sent out by the harmful person be returned to them, but also that they will look into those mirrors and truly see and know the full gravity of their behavior. Hold this visualization as strongly as you can for as long as possible and then release the energy to them all at once. Will the force to surround them until they truly accept responsibility for what they do and then end the exercise.

THIRTEEN

Weather Magic

In the distant past, it is said that Witches were known to "whistle up the wind" or to tie the wind into knotted cords and when they wished to change the weather, the cord could be untied to release the energy. There are many other methods of weather working, as it is known since forecasting future weather patterns and control over those forces have been coveted practices since humankind's early days. According to Frazer's *Golden Bough*, weather magic is frequently (though not always) worked through the use of imitative (sympathetic) magic. This is still true, though the methods he describes as being used by "primitive" tribes such as wrapping crystals in emu feathers or three people climbing in trees of a sacred grove to drum, ignite sparks and sprinkle water to encourage rainfall are a bit cumbersome and difficult to perform on an as needed basis. Today, simpler methods have been devised that preserve the same intent while maintaining greater ease of use.

Is This Ethical?

In more recent times, weather magic tends to be frowned upon by much of the magical community who considers it tampering with the fragile balance of nature, potentially creating devastating consequences. The argument goes that in order to shift the weather in your area, patterns of flow are diverted that cause shifts throughout the globe and these shifts could cause climate changes that result in storms, tornadoes, hail, etc.

While it is true that causing a shift in one area will have a domino effect that ripples outward creating changes everywhere—this is the way all magic works—simple rites designed to change the weather can be worked without unleashing harmful unintended side effects if proper precautions are taken.

Weather Working

Before undertaking the actual practice of weather magic, it is a wise idea to familiarize yourself with basic knowledge of meteorology. I'm not saying you need to have a degree in it; learning the fundamentals of weather, air currents, the water cycle, high pressure systems, low pressure systems, humidity, barometric pressure, and other natural phenomena are quite useful. When we know what atmospheric factors we are dealing with, influencing them becomes much easier. What follows is a very rudimentary look at weather patterns.

A strong driving force behind the weather of our planet is the sun's radiation. The sun's energy heats the earth's atmosphere, but due to the planet's rotation and tilt, heat is not evenly distributed; if the areas are warmer, a warmer air mass forms. In a cooler area, a cold air mass develops since the temperature of an air mass is influenced by surface heat (or lack thereof). The differing temperature of the air creates either high pressure or low pressure. Ironically when the air is warmer, since heat expands and rises, the air molecules move higher in the atmosphere reducing their density and resulting in a low pressure system. Since this air is moving high and away from the surface, the air closer to the surface rushes in to take its place to avoid creating a vacuum. This movement of air is what causes wind, cool surface air, and the bringing in of clouds and why a low pressure system is associated with colder temperatures, unstable weather, and precipitation.

In a high pressure system, the opposite is true: the air remains dense and close to the surface, usually resulting is more stable conditions and warmer weather, sunny days, and no wind. High and low pressure systems play off each other and when combined with the planet's surface friction and rotation, result in the movement of the weather patterns in a manner known as the Coriolis effect. In the northern hemisphere, the effect results in a counterclockwise swirl of movement; in the southern hemisphere, it causes a clockwise swirl. This action is seen most profoundly in the swirl of hurricanes.

There is much more to learn about weather but this is enough to begin. Basically the magic covered here is designed to release intention into the already established pattern and encourage its shift toward our goal. We are not seeking to "create" the desired weather but rather the conditions for it to manifest naturally. Whether one is seeking a long term weather change such as a week of warm weather in the middle of winter or a short term effect of a single nice day for an outdoor ritual, any weather magic must be cast with the caveat that the spell shall be "with harm to none and for the good of all" because adding this intention into the working will help mitigate any negative consequences.

For Rain

There are various herbs and tools used to encourage rain. Three of the most often used herbs are henbane (very poisonous), ferns, and heather. In some instances these are burned but a safer method for rain magic is to omit the henbane and use the other two herbs in the spell.

Stirring the Rain

Use a large sprig of heather, a large bunch of fern leaves, a combination of both tied together as a makeshift besom (ritual broom) or use your usual ritual broom if you have one, for this rite. If possible, go to a natural source of water such as a river for this working. If that is impossible, it can be done in a yard with a basin of water or even in a bathtub (carefully). Use the herbs or broom to gently stir the water while visualizing a falling rain.

Next, lift up the broom and sprinkle water into each cardinal direction, making sure to feel it falling on your skin while you ask for rain to fall. Any form of weather actually involves all four elements, so it is appropriate to call upon them with words such as these: "Earth, fire, wind, and sea; shift the patterns, bring rain to me." If you have used herbs for this spell, you can allow them to dry and burn them safely in a cauldron or fireplace to add to the spell's power. If a broom was used, simply dry it off and put it away.

For Sun

If the day is cloudy and you are seeking sunshine, there are two simple methods for creating a break in the clouds. The first one is to pour a cup of water into a cauldron and add two table-spoons of salt. Bring the water to a boil, and as it boils away, visualize that the water and steam are the clouds and moisture blocking the sun. Send this mental image upward to the sky. After most of the water has been evaporated, turn off the heat and let the cauldron cool. As soon as the cauldron has cooled, thoroughly wash it—salt corrodes metal.

The second method to see the sun involves magically affect-ing the wind so it blows the clouds away.

For Wind

A classic method for crafting wind is through the use of a knot-ted cord. This cord must be prepared ahead of time and saved until needed. To create a Wind Cord, use a length of white rope made of natural fibers about one foot in length. On a windy day, go outside holding the cord and let the wind touch its surface. Visualize the energy of the wind being absorbed into the fibers of the cord. When you feel ready, tie a knot in one end of the cord, trapping some of the energy. Say something like, "I capture the wind in this knot, its full force is hereby caught" as you tie the cord. Tie a second knot in the other end and say, "Twice the strength with knot of two, in this cord the wind comes through." Tie the third and final knot in the middle of the cord saying, "Knot of three binds triple the strength, charging the cord along its length and when unleashed, winds shall blow and the power of air shall freely flow."

Once created, coil up the cord and wrap it in silk or cotton fabric, storing it away until needed. To use the cord, go outside holding the cord and visualize the idea of wind; the way it feels against the skin, tree branches dancing in the breeze, leaves drifting through the air. As you hold your visualization, untie the first knot. You don't have to undo all three knots. The tradition says to untie one for a breeze, two for a strong wind, and all three for a gale (be careful with that last one!).

For Snow

Cast a circle and sit in the center. Go into a meditative state and call upon the element of water. Visualize the energy of water emerging from the west quarter and traveling upward, all the way to the sky, bringing icy cold, clouds, and snow. Mentally concentrate the power of water into a dense form; visualize the water energy crystallizing into shimmering snowflakes and that they begin to fall. Kindle your emotions and all your senses through your visualization; "feel" the snow touch your skin, see it falling in your mind's eye, hear the flakes falling through tree branches, and taste and smell that distinctive change in the air when rain or snow arrives. Once your visualization has peaked, release all the energy outward to the sky, and end the rite.

PART THREE
Ingredients & Recipes

Here are the recipes for the oils and incenses in the spells appearing in this book. In all recipes, any herbs listed are to be used in their dried form and the instructions remain the same unless otherwise noted. To create incense, grind the herbs and other dry ingredients together first before adding any liquids. Spread the mixture on a plate and allow it to completely dry before charging and storing for use. To create an oil, warm the base oil in a pot over very low heat and add the charged herbs to the pot, swirling them in the oil one at a time. Once you can smell the herbs in the air, remove the oil from the heat and allow it to cool before straining, bottling, and charging for use.

FOURTEEN

Magical Recipe Book

Attraction Oil (female attracting)

1 tablespoon each, dried and ground:

- Cinnamon

- Nutmeg

- Ginger

- Cardamom

- ½ cup vegetable oil

Add a ¼ teaspoon fresh vanilla or ½ teaspoon vanilla extract. (Note: if using vanilla extract, the finished oil will have to be shaken before each use to blend.)

Attraction Oil (male attracting)
1 tablespoon each, dried and ground:

- Cinnamon
- Ginger
- Nutmeg
- Allspice
- Cloves
- Lavender flowers
- ½ cup vegetable oil

Binding Oil
1 tablespoon each, dried:

- Ivy
- Periwinkle (leaves and flowers)
- Mullein
- ½ cup vegetable oil

Binding Incense
1 tablespoon each, dried:

- Mullein
- Sage
- Nettle
- 2 drops binding oil

Healing Oil

1 tablespoon each:

- Red carnation petals
- Myrrh
- Hops
- ½ cup olive oil

Healing Incense

1 tablespoon each, dried:

- Angelica
- Peppermint
- Bay leaves
- 2 drops healing oil

Love Oil

1 tablespoon each:

- Red rose petals
- Marjoram
- Yarrow
- ½ cup olive oil

Love Incense

1 tablespoon each, dried:

- Basil

- Marjoram

- Catnip

Love Potion

Ingredients are listed below:

- 2 cups spring water

- 1 tablespoon dried basil

- 1 tablespoon dried red rose petals

- 1 teaspoon vanilla extract

Money Oil

1 tablespoon each:

- Heliotrope

- Cinnamon

- Red clover seeds

- Fenugreek seeds

- ½ cup almond oil

Money Incense

1 tablespoon each, dried:

- Sage

- Cinnamon

- ¼ teaspoon orange zest

- Pinch whole wheat flour

Persuasion Oil
1 tablespoon each:

- Rosemary
- Licorice root
- Damiana
- Jojoba or olive oil

Persuasion Incense
1 tablespoon each:

- Rosemary
- Licorice
- Bergamot

Protection Oil
1 tablespoon each:

- Sage
- Rosemary
- Dill
- 1 crushed garlic clove
- ½ cup olive oil

Protection Incense
1 tablespoon each, dried:

- Frankincense

- Myrrh

- Vervain

- 2 drops protection oil

Planetary Oils

1 tablespoon of each herb to the chosen oil:

Sun

- Bay

- Juniper

- Carnation flowers

- ½ cup olive oil

Mercury

- Caraway seeds

- Dill

- Marjoram

- ½ cup almond oil

Venus

- Catnip

- Cardamom

- Daffodil

- ½ cup olive oil

Moon

- Coconut flakes
- Lemon zest
- Poppy seeds
- ½ cup grapeseed oil

Mars

- Basil
- Ginger
- Nettle
- ½ cup vegetable oil

Jupiter

- Cinquefoil
- Dandelion
- Nutmeg
- Sage
- ½ cup vegetable oil

Saturn

- Comfrey
- Ivy
- Mullein
- ¼ teaspoon beet juice
- ½ cup vegetable oil

Uranus

- Peppermint
- Clovers
- Pomegranate seeds
- ½ cup vegetable oil

Neptune

- Poppy seeds
- Chamomile
- Coffee beans
- ½ cup grape seed oil

Pluto

- Black cohosh
- Rye
- Ginger
- ½ cup vegetable oil

Polaris Oil (North Star)

1 tablespoon each, powdered:

- Frankincense
- Myrrh
- ½ cup vegetable oil

Fomalhaut Oil (Watcher of the North)

1 tablespoon each:

- White bryony (poisonous, substitute hops)
- Poke root
- Peppermint
- ½ cup almond oil

Regulus Oil (Watcher of the South)

1 tablespoon each:

- Angelica
- Benzoin
- Calamus
- Chamomile
- ½ cup olive oil

Aldebaran Oil (Watcher of the East)

1 tablespoon each:

- Benzoin
- Sage
- Lemon grass
- Lavender
- ½ cup olive oil

Antares Oil (Watcher of the West)

1 tablespoon each:

- Hazel nuts, crushed

- Poppy seeds

- White rose petals, dried

- ½ cup almond oil

Planetary Incenses

1 tablespoon of each herb, dried unless otherwise noted.

Sun

- Rosemary

- Orange zest

- Bay leaves

Mercury

- Dill

- Lemongrass

- Marjoram

- Venus

- Cardamom

- Spearmint

- Thyme

Moon

- Lemon zest
- Myrrh
- Lemongrass
- Bay leaves

Mars

- Allspice
- Basil
- Peppermint
- Nettle

Jupiter

- Anise
- Sage
- Nutmeg

Saturn

- Mullein
- Myrrh
- 1 pinch tobacco (optional)

Uranus

- Peppermint
- Rue
- Summer savory

Neptune

- Grape leaves
- Kelp
- Chamomile

Pluto

- Wild mint
- Wormwood
- 1 pinch ginger

Polaris Incense (North Star)

1 tablespoon each, dried and powdered:

- Frankincense
- Myrrh
- Juniper berries

Fomalhaut Incense (Watcher of the North)

1 tablespoon each, dried:

- Jasmine flowers
- Peppermint

Regulus Incense (Watcher of the South)

1 tablespoon each, dried:

- Gum arabic
- Cinnamon

- Bay leaves, crushed

- Orange peel, grated

Aldebaran Incense (Watcher of the East)

1 tablespoon each, dried:

- Marjoram

- Benzoin

- Pinch of powdered cloves

Antares Incense (Watcher of the West)

1 tablespoon each, dried:

- Wormwood

- White sandalwood

- White rose petals

Latin Names of Herbs Used in These Recipes:

- **Almond:** *Prunus dulcis*

- **Allspice:** *Pimenta dioica*

- **Angelica:** *Angelica archangelica*

- **Anise:** *Pimpinella anisum*

- **Basil:** *Ocimum basilicum*

- **Bay:** *Laurus nobilis*

- **Beet:** *Beta vulgaris*

- **Benzoin:** *Styrax benzoin*

- **Black cohosh:** *Actaea racemosa*
- **Blue cohosh:** *Caulophyllum thalictroides*
- **Calamus:** *Acorus calamus*
- **Carnation:** *Dianthus caryophyllus*
- **Caraway:** *Carum carvi*
- **Cardamom:** *Elettaria cardamomum*
- **Catnip:** *Nepeta cateria*
- **Chamomile:** *Anthemis nobilis*
- **Cinnamon:** *Cinnamonium spp.*
- **Cinquefoil:** *Potentilla reptans*
- **Clove:** *Syzygium aromaticum*
- **Clover:** *Trifolium spp.*
- **Coconut:** *Cocos nucifera*
- **Coffee:** *Coffea arabica (C. robusta)*
- **Comfrey:** *Symphytum officinalis*
- **Daffodil:** *Narcissus pseudonarcissus*
- **Dandelion:** *Taraxicum officinalis*
- **Dill:** *Anethum graveolens*
- **Fenugreek:** *Trigonella foenum-graecum*
- **Frankincense:** *Boswellia spp.*
- **Garlic:** *Allium sativa*
- **Grape:** *Vitis vinifera*

- **Ginger:** *Zingiber officinalis*

- **Gum arabic:** *Acacia senegal*

- **Hazel:** *Corylus spp.*

- **Heliotrope:** *Heliotropium arborescens*

- **Hops:** *Humulus lupulus*

- **Ivy:** *Hedera helix*

- **Jasmine:** *Jasminum spp.*

- **Juniper:** *Juniperus communis*

- **Kelp (bladderwrack):** *Fucus vesiculosus*

- **Lavender:** *Lavandula spp.*

- **Lemon:** *Citrus limon*

- **Lemongrass:** *Cymbopogon spp.*

- **Marjoram:** *Origanum majorana*

- **Mugwort:** *Artemisia vulgaris*

- **Mullein:** *Verbascum thapsus*

- **Myrrh:** *Commiphora myrrha* (or *C. molmol*)

- **Nettle:** *Urtica spp.*

- **Nutmeg:** *Myristica fragrans*

- **Orange:** *Citrus sinensis*

- **Pennyroyal:** *Hedeoma pulegiodes*

- **Peppermint:** *Mentha piperita*

- **Periwinkle:** *Vinca (major or minor)*

- **Poke root:** *Phytolacca spp.*

- **Pomegranate:** *Punica granatum*

- **Poppy seeds:** *Papaver somniferum*

- **Red clover:** *Trifolium pretense*

- **Rose:** *Rosa spp.*

- **Rosemary:** *Rosmarinus officinalis*

- **Rue:** *Ruta graveolens*

- **Sage:** *Salvia officinalis*

- **Sandalwood:** *Santalum spp.*

- **Spearmint:** *Mentha spicata*

- **Summer savory:** *Satureja hortensis*

- **Thyme:** *Thymus vulgaris*

- **Tobacco:** *Nicotiana tabacum*

- **Vanilla:** *Vanilla planifolia*

- **Vervain:** *Verbena officinalis*

- **Wormseed:** *Artemisia cina*

- **Wormwood:** *Artemisia absinthium*

- **Yarrow:** *Achillea millefolium*

Bibliography

Buckland, Raymond. *Signs, Symbols, and Omens: An Illustrated Guide to Magical and Spiritual Symbolism.* St. Paul, MN: Llewellyn Publications, 2003.

———. *Buckland's Complete Book of Witchcraft.* St. Paul, MN: Llewellyn Publications, 1986, 2002.

Cabot, Laurie. *Power of the Witch: The Earth, The Moon, and the Magical Path to Enlightenment.* New York: Delta, 1989.

———. *Love Magic: The Way to Love Through Rituals, Spells, and the Magical Life.* New York: Delta, 1992.

Cunningham, Scott. *Wicca: A Guide for the Solitary Practitioner.* St. Paul, MN: Llewellyn Publications, 1994.

———. *Cunningham's Encyclopedia of Magical Herbs.* St. Paul, MN: Llewellyn Publications, 1985.

De Angeles, Ly. *Witchcraft: Theory and Practice*. St. Paul, MN: Llewellyn Publications, 2000.

Dugan, Ellen. *Herb Magic for Beginners: Down to Earth Enchantments*. St. Paul, MN: Llewellyn Publications, 2006.

Eason, Cassandra. *A Complete Guide to Night Magic*. New York: Citadel Press, 2002.

Fitch, Ed. *A Grimoire of Shadows: Witchcraft, Paganism, and Magick*. St. Paul, MN: Llewellyn Publications, 1996.

Frazer, Sir James George. *The Golden Bough: A Study in Magic and Religion*. London: Oxford University Press, 2009.

Furie, Michael. *Spellcasting for Beginners: A Simple Guide to Magical Practice*. Woodbury, MN: Llewellyn Publications, 2012.

———. *Supermarket Magic: Creating Spells, Brews, Potions, and Powders from Everyday Ingredients*. Woodbury, MN: Llewellyn Publications, 2013.

Grimassi, Raven. *The Witches' Craft*. St. Paul, MN: Llewellyn Publications, 2002.

———. *Wiccan Magick: Inner Teachings of the Craft*. St. Paul, MN: Llewellyn Publications, 2002.

———. *Hereditary Witchcraft: Secrets of the Old Religion:* St. Paul, MN: Llewellyn Publications, 1999.

Illes, Judika. *Pure Magic: A Complete Course in Spellcasting.* San Francisco: Weiser, 2007.

Martello, Dr. Leo Louis. *Witchcraft: The Old Religion.* New York: Kensington Publishing, 1998.

Miller, Susan. *Planets and Possibilities: Explore the Worlds Beyond Your Sun Sign.* New York: Warner Books, 2001.

Paddon, Peter. *Enchantment: The Witch's Art of Manipulation Through Gesture, Gaze, and Glamour.* Los Angeles: Pendraig Publishing, 2013.

Three Initiates. *The Kybalion: A Study of the Hermetic Philosophy of Ancient Egypt and Greece.* London: White Crane Publishing, 2011. First published 1908 by the Yogi Publication Society.

Weinstein, Marion. *Earth Magic: A Dianic Book of Shadows.* New York: Earth Magic Productions, 1986.

Index

GET MORE AT LLEWELLYN.COM

Visit us online to browse hundreds of our books and decks, plus sign up to receive our e-newsletters and exclusive online offers.

- **• Free tarot readings • Spell-a-Day • Moon phases**
- **• Recipes, spells, and tips • Blogs • Encyclopedia**
- **• Author interviews, articles, and upcoming events**

GET SOCIAL WITH LLEWELLYN

Find us on Facebook
www.Facebook.com/LlewellynBooks

Follow us on

www.Twitter.com/Llewellynbooks

GET BOOKS AT LLEWELLYN

LLEWELLYN ORDERING INFORMATION

Order online: Visit our website at www.llewellyn.com to select your books and place an order on our secure server.

Order by phone:
- Call toll free within the U.S. at 1-877-NEW-WRLD (1-877-639-9753)
- Call toll free within Canada at 1-866-NEW-WRLD (1-866-639-9753)
- We accept VISA, MasterCard, and American Express

Order by mail:
Send the full price of your order (MN residents add 6.875% sales tax) in U.S. funds, plus postage and handling to: Llewellyn Worldwide, 2143 Wooddale Drive, Woodbury, MN 55125-2989

POSTAGE AND HANDLING:

STANDARD: (U.S. & Canada)
(Please allow 12 business days)
$25.00 and under, add $4.00.
$25.01 and over, FREE SHIPPING.

INTERNATIONAL ORDERS (airmail only):
$16.00 for one book, plus $3.00 for each additional book.

Visit us online for more shipping options. Prices subject to change.

FREE CATALOG!

To order, call
1-877-
NEW-WRLD
ext. 8236
or visit our
website

Spellcasting for Beginners
A Simple Guide to Magical Practice
MICHAEL FURIE

With accessible descriptions of magical techniques, Michael Furie teaches you the practical use of over seventy simple spells and rituals. *Spellcasting for Beginners* includes the basic skills of creating intention and projecting energy, and shows how to integrate them into essential spells for love, healing, money, bringing forth visions, creating blessings, and more. You'll also learn about magical ethics, correspondences, magical tools, and how to design your own spells.

Work with Michael as he describes how to meditate, raise energy, and focus on specific results of spellwork. Create a basic altar for solitary practice, learn to create magical recipes with natural ingredients, experiment with nature-based magic, and discover the wonderful uses of crystals, gems, and charms. Practitioners will continue to refer to *Spellcasting for Beginners* even after moving out of the beginning stage.

978-0-7387-3309-8, 264 pp., 5³⁄₁₆ x 8   **$13.99**

Creating Spells, Brews, Potions & Powders
from Everyday Ingredients

SUPERMARKET
MAGIC

MICHAEL FURIE

Supermarket Magic
Creating Spells, Brews, Potions
& Powders from Everyday Ingredients
Michael Furie

The tools of magic don't have to be expensive or difficult to find—they're right in your supermarket aisles! This easy-to-use book provides clear instructions for working simple and powerful spells—with only common ingredients.

Perfect for Witches and all practitioners of natural and herbal magic, this essential guide explains all the basics of magic including ethics, meditation, timing, and basic charging techniques. There are clear instructions for working a wide variety of simple and powerful spells: clearing and cleaning, increasing harmony, healing, love, lust, beauty, luck money, protection, and honing psychic abilities. Discover how to whip up magical brews, powders, and oils using inexpensive items that can be conveniently purchased at your local grocery store.

978-0-7387-3655-6, 288 pp., 5³⁄₁₆ x 8   **$15.99**

Practical Magick Series

RAY BUCKLAND

ADVANCED
CANDLE MAGICK

MORE SPELLS AND RITUALS FOR EVERY PURPOSE

Advanced Candle Magick
More Spells and Rituals for Every Purpose
Ray Buckland

Seize control of your destiny with the simple but profound practice of *Advanced Candle Magick*. Ray Buckland's first book on candle magick *Practical Candleburning Rituals* explained the basic techniques of directing positive forces and making things happen. In *Advanced Candle Magick*, you'll use advanced spells, preparatory work, visualization and astrology to improve and enhance your results. Create a framework conducive to potent spellwork through the use of planetary hours, days of the week, herb and stone correspondences, and color symbolism. Create positive changes in your relationships, finances, health and spirit when you devise your own powerful rituals based upon the sample spells presented in this book. Taking spellworking one step further, Ray Buckland gives you what you've been waiting for: *Advanced Candle Magick*.

978-1-56718-1036, 288 pp., 5¼ x 8 **$15.99**